DIFFERENTIATION *and* THE BRAIN

How Neuroscience Supports the Learner-Friendly Classroom

DAVID A.
SOUSA

CAROL ANN
TOMLINSON

Solution Tree | Press

a division of

Solution Tree

555 North Morton Street
Bloomington, IN 47404
800.733.6786 (toll free) / 812.336.7700
FAX: 812.336.7790

email: info@solution-tree.com
solution-tree.com

Visit **go.solution-tree.com/instruction** to download the reproducibles in this book.

Printed in the United States of America

14 13   5

Library of Congress Cataloging-in-Publication Data

Sousa, David A.
  Differentiation and the brain : how neuroscience supports the learner-friendly classroom / David A. Sousa, Carol Ann Tomlinson.
     p. cm.
  Includes bibliographical references and index.
  ISBN 978-1-935249-59-7 (perfect bound) -- ISBN 978-1-935249-60-3 (library ed.) 1. Individualized instruction--Psychological aspects. 2. Learning, Psychology of. 3. Brain. 4. Neurosciences. I. Tomlinson, Carol A. II. Title.
  LB1031.S65 2011
  371.39'4019--dc22
                    2010023332

Solution Tree
Jeffrey C. Jones, CEO & President

Solution Tree Press
President: Douglas M. Rife
Publisher: Robert D. Clouse
Vice President of Production: Gretchen Knapp
Managing Production Editor: Caroline Wise
Senior Production Editor: Risë Koben
Proofreader: Rachel Rosolina
Text Designer: Amy Shock
Cover Designer: Orlando Angel

Acknowledgments

Solution Tree Press would like to thank the following reviewers:

Travis Brady
Social Studies Educator
Southwest High School
Lincoln, Nebraska

Diane Heacox
Associate Professor of Education
St. Catherine University
St. Paul, Minnesota

Eric Jensen
President
Jensen Learning
Maunaloa, Hawaii

Patrick Smith
Science Teacher
Rogers High School
Rogers, Arkansas

Judy Willis
Author and Consultant
Santa Barbara, California

Rick Wormeli
Author and Consultant
Herndon, Virginia

Visit **go.solution-tree.com/instruction** to download the
reproducibles in this book.

Table of Contents

Italicized entries indicate reproducible pages.

3 Curriculum and Differentiation **45**

4 Classroom Assessment and Differentiation **63**

About the Authors

 **David A. Sousa, EdD,** is an international consultant in educational neuroscience and author of more than a dozen books that suggest ways that educators and parents can translate current brain research into strategies for improving learning. He has made presentations to more than one hundred thousand educators across the United States, Canada, Europe, Australia, New Zealand, and Asia.

Dr. Sousa has a bachelor's degree in chemistry from Massachusetts State College at Bridgewater, a master of arts in teaching degree in science from Harvard University, and a doctorate from Rutgers University. He has taught senior high school science and has served as a K–12 director of science and a district superintendent in New Jersey schools. He has been an adjunct professor of education at Seton Hall University and a visiting lecturer at Rutgers University.

Dr. Sousa has edited science books and published dozens of articles in leading journals on staff development, science education, and educational research. His most popular books for educators include *How the Brain Learns*, third edition; *How the Special Needs Brain Learns*, second edition; *How the Gifted Brain Learns*; *How the Brain Learns to Read*; *How the Brain Influences Behavior*; *How the Brain Learns Mathematics*, which was selected by the Independent Publishers' Association as one of the best professional development books of 2008; *The Leadership Brain*; and *Mind, Brain, and Education: Neuroscience Implications for the Classroom*. His books have been published in French, Spanish, Chinese, Arabic, and several other languages.

Dr. Sousa is past president of the National Staff Development Council. He has received numerous awards, including the Distinguished Alumni Award and an honorary doctorate from Massachusetts State College at Bridgewater and an honorary doctorate from Gratz College in Philadelphia.

Dr. Sousa has been interviewed by Matt Lauer on NBC's *TODAY* and by National Public Radio about his work with schools using brain research. He makes his home in south Florida.

Carol Ann Tomlinson, EdD, is a faculty member at the University of Virginia's Curry School of Education, where she is the William Clay Parrish Jr. Professor and chair of the Department of Educational Leadership, Foundations, and Policy. Dr. Tomlinson codirects the university's Institutes on Academic Diversity. She was named Outstanding Professor in the Curry School of Education in 2004 and received an All University Teaching Award in 2008.

As a consultant, trainer, and presenter, Dr. Tomlinson works with teachers throughout the United States and internationally to develop more responsive, heterogeneous classrooms. Her education experience includes twenty-one years as a public school teacher and twelve years as a program administrator of special services for struggling and advanced learners.

During her time in the public school classroom, Dr. Tomlinson was recognized by the state of Virginia as Teacher of the Year. She has focused on a number of critical issues throughout her career, including curriculum and instruction for struggling and advanced learners, effective instruction in heterogeneous settings, and encouraging creative and critical thinking in the classroom.

Dr. Tomlinson is a reviewer for eight journals and the author of more than two hundred articles, book chapters, books, and professional development materials. Among her books on differentiation are: *How to Differentiate Instruction in Mixed-Ability Classrooms, The Differentiated Classroom: Responding to the Needs of all Learners, Fulfilling the Promise of the Differentiated Classroom: Strategies and Tools for Responsive Teaching, Integrating Differentiated Instruction and Understanding by Design: Connecting Content and Kids* (with Jay McTighe), and *Leading and Managing a Differentiated Classroom* (with Marcia Imbeau). Her books on differentiation have been translated into twelve languages. She has a bachelor's degree from the University of South Carolina and a master's degree and doctor of education degree from the University of Virginia.

Introduction

With more than a hundred books already available on differentiation, why do we need this one? That is a fair question, and here is our answer. To our knowledge, this book is different from all the others in that it combines two imperatives that face nearly all educators today:

1. Research is revealing so much about how the brain learns that educators can no longer ignore the implications of these discoveries for educational practice.

2. Teachers need to find ways to use this brain research to develop strategies that will allow students to succeed in classrooms that contain a diverse mix of abilities, cultures, and languages.

The discoveries from neuroscientific research that can affect educational practice have accumulated since the 1980s and are now to the point where a whole new and exciting discipline has emerged. It is called *educational neuroscience*, and it brings together related research from cognitive psychology, neuroscience, and pedagogy. This research pool offers information and insights that can help educators decide whether certain curricular, instructional, and assessment choices are likely to be more effective than others. In this book, we examine the basic principles of differentiation in light of what the current research has revealed, and the result is surprisingly positive, indeed. We wanted to share those surprises with the reader.

> In this book, we examine the basic principles of differentiation in light of current research, and the result is surprisingly positive, indeed.

How Brain-Friendly Is Differentiation?

As authors and longtime educators, we have focused on somewhat different areas of educational practice. One of us has been intimately involved in developing frameworks for establishing differentiated classrooms at all grade levels and subject areas—and teaching in them. The other has investigated how the findings from cognitive and neuroscientific research could be translated into what educators do in schools and classrooms. When we discussed the possibilities for this book, we recognized that the processes for differentiating curriculum, instruction, and assessment were supported in many ways by what researchers in cognitive psychology and neuroscience were revealing about how the brain learns. In other words, differentiation is brain-friendly and brain-compatible.

The Rise, Fall, and Rise of Differentiation

Differentiation is not a new idea. Think back to the one-room schoolhouse of the late nineteenth and early twentieth centuries, where one teacher had to educate children of varying ages and grade levels at the same time in a single classroom. That teacher had to be an expert in differentiating curriculum, instructional strategies, and assessment techniques. Using only a few resources—chalk, a slate, and some books—the students learned literacy, arithmetic, penmanship, and good manners. In this environment, the students and teacher were often together for several years in a row, so they got to know each other very well. This close relationship allowed the teacher to tailor instruction for an individual student. No doubt, the seeds of cooperative learning sprouted here, too, as older students helped the younger ones. (More than three hundred one-room schoolhouses still exist across rural America.)

As the population grew, public schools got bigger. Students were separated into single grade levels, according to their age. Class size was small, and John Dewey's notion of a school as a caring community encouraged teachers to address the needs of individual students. Curriculum decisions were made locally and reflected the needs of the community. Some towns wanted their students to have more academic subjects, while others focused on developing their students' vocational and agricultural skills. Differentiated classrooms were still common.

Although students within a grade level still demonstrated varying degrees of ability and maturity, the prevailing and powerful industrial model began to shape educational philosophy and school operations in the 1930s. Within this organizational structure, differentiation in the classroom yielded to the seemingly more efficient middle-of-the-road approach. Academic subjects were departmentalized, class sizes grew even larger, and secondary-level teachers became content specialists. Differentiation faltered when the one-size-fits-all curriculum emerged as the common basis for instruction.

> While school districts were becoming more *alike* in their curriculum, instruction, and assessment practices, the school population was becoming more *diverse*.

Because of fears that local school districts still had too much autonomy and variation, in the 1960s the states began to exert more control over their operations. State departments of education generated curriculum standards and developed standardized tests that nearly all students had to take to graduate high school. Meanwhile, the immigrant population mushroomed, bringing more languages and cultures into the society, and urban flight widened the economic gap between neighboring communities. So, while school districts across the country were becoming more *alike* in their curriculum, instruction, and assessment practices, the school population was becoming more *diverse*.

For years, nationwide test results showed only modest—if any—gains in student achievement across the grades. Secondary students in the United States continued to score lower than students in most other developed countries. In an attempt to improve performance, policymakers called for reforms that put even more emphasis on standards and testing (for example, the No Child Left Behind Act). In the face of these pressures to standardize, educators came to realize that the one-size-fits-all approach does not succeed with many students in today's classrooms. It became evident that the broad range of abilities, languages, and cultures in our schools requires teachers to incorporate different levels of instruction within the same classroom—a return, to some degree, to the diverse strategies of the one-room school. The idea of differentiation was reborn.

About This Book

Some school districts have long sought ways to maintain differentiation in their classrooms despite the driving forces of unreasonable amounts of content to cover and the accompanying high-stakes testing. As policymakers and communities continue to recognize the growing diversity of their student population, more schools will turn to differentiation to help this broad mix of students succeed. In this book, we offer suggestions on how to establish and manage differentiated classrooms without imposing additional heavy burdens on teachers. We talk about teaching *differently* and *smarter*, not *harder*. In fact, when properly implemented, differentiation emphasizes shared responsibility between teacher and student—a desirable outcome, because the brain that does the work is the brain that learns!

> Differentiation emphasizes shared responsibility between teacher and student, because the brain that does the work is the brain that learns!

Questions This Book Will Answer

This book will answer questions such as these:

- What kind of model can teachers use as a basis for setting up a differentiated and brain-friendly classroom?

- How do the mindsets of teachers and students affect differentiation?

- What kind of learning environment is most conducive to differentiation?

- What are the five major components of a brain-friendly quality curriculum?

- What are effective practices for assessing student achievement to inform instruction?

- What is meant by student readiness, and how do teachers respond to it?

- How important are student interests in the differentiated classroom, and how are they handled?

- What are the components of learning profiles, and how do teachers plan for them?

- What are some strategies for effectively managing the differentiated classroom?

Chapter Contents

Chapter 1: The Nonnegotiables of Effective Differentiation—In this chapter, we describe differentiation and its research base. We present a model that incorporates the basic elements of a differentiated classroom and give a brief overview of the model's parts that will be discussed in greater detail in succeeding chapters.

Chapter 2: Mindset, Learning Environment, and Differentiation—Here we explore different types of teacher and student mindsets and how they may affect teaching and learning. We describe the impact of the classroom and school environment on body chemistry as well as on social needs and other factors that affect student learning.

Chapter 3: Curriculum and Differentiation—This chapter deals primarily with the five important components of a brain-friendly quality curriculum. We discuss each component and suggest ways that it can be implemented in a differentiated classroom.

Chapter 4: Classroom Assessment and Differentiation—Because assessment is such an integral part of teaching and learning, we devote this chapter to examining the nature and purposes of assessment. We focus particularly on assessment strategies that are more likely to be effective because they take into account the diversity among learners.

Chapter 5: Differentiating in Response to Student Readiness—Student readiness is often equated with student ability, but they are not the same. In this chapter, we explain the differences, discuss why readiness matters, and offer suggestions for responding to student readiness through the learning environment as well as through curriculum, assessment, and management strategies.

Chapter 6: Differentiating in Response to Student Interest—How much interest a person has in learning something is a key factor in that person's motivation to learn and his or her subsequent achievement. Here we state why addressing students' interests can make for challenging, rewarding, and successful learning activities. We include suggestions for taking students' interests into account when supporting the learning environment and when planning curriculum, assessment, and management strategies.

Chapter 7: Differentiating in Response to Student Learning Profile— Although teachers are aware that students learn in different ways, planning for these differences on a day-to-day basis may seem impractical. But that is not the case. In this chapter, we describe some of the components of learning profiles, the variables that affect learning profiles, and some guidelines that teachers can use to plan for different learning profiles.

Chapter 8: Managing a Differentiated Classroom—Our suggestions in the previous chapters may at first seem overwhelming, but with careful and thoughtful planning, the teacher can implement them in productive ways. This chapter helps with that careful and thoughtful planning. It explores the differences between leadership and management and suggests how teachers can use their leadership skills to move students through challenging and exciting learning opportunities in a differentiated learning environment.

Other Helpful Tools

A Case in Point and **A Better Scenario:** These vignettes appear in chapters 2 through 8. Positioned at the beginnings of these chapters, "A Case in Point" describes situations in a typical classroom. At the chapter conclusions, "A Better Scenario" describes how the classroom situations might improve if the teacher planned for the differentiation component discussed in that chapter. Our hope is that these vignettes will demonstrate how using the suggested strategies could make for a positive and productive learning environment and success for students.

In the Classroom: These scenarios are intended to help educators envision how various aspects of differentiation, including specific instructional strategies, might look in action in specific, brain-friendly classroom settings.

Exercises: In nearly every chapter we offer questions for reflection along with multiple suggestions about how to design and implement strategies associated with the topic discussed in that chapter. These questions and suggestions come not only from the psychological and neuroscientific research but also from research on the best educational practices associated with differentiation and brain-compatible instruction.

As we gain a greater understanding of how the human brain learns, we may discover ways to better meet the needs of our increasingly diverse student population. Sometimes, students are attempting to learn in environments that are designed to help but instead inadvertently hinder their efforts. By looking for ways to differentiate the instruction and change some of our assessment approaches, we may be able to help more students achieve their full potential. We understand the considerable imperfections that are part of many teaching environments. We know that teachers long for smaller class sizes, larger rooms, more materials, more time for planning, and more relevant professional support. We are keenly aware of—and saddened by— the unremitting pressure to raise test scores. We also know, however, that those realities may outlive us all. In the end, young lives are enriched and enlivened by teachers who say, "These are my students. This is the only time they will ever experience this grade/these subjects. I understand both the opportunity and the responsibility that this presents to me. I will see these students as three-dimensional human beings. I will learn about them. I will continue to sharpen the art and science of my work so that I can teach them the best possible content in the best possible ways. I will do whatever I can in this time and place to support the success of each student who comes to me."

Our hope is that this book will encourage all school professionals to learn more about how the brain learns and about approaches to differentiation so that we can work together for the benefit of all students. In other words, we hope this book will help teachers sharpen their knowledge of the science that illuminates the art of effective teaching and will inspire them to use that knowledge to benefit the students they teach.

CHAPTER 1

The Nonnegotiables of Effective Differentiation

It seems awkward to even have to discuss the idea of differentiating curriculum and instruction to meet the needs of different kinds of learners, but the reality is that too many classrooms are still teaching with the focus of "one for all and all for one." No one would deny that children learn in different ways and with different amounts of time on task, but traditional school structures, pressures of content coverage for standardized tests, and limited budgets for staff development make the idea of differentiating to maximize learning a mountain still to be climbed. But we must [climb it]. . . .

—H. Lynn Erickson, *Stirring the Head, Heart, and Soul*

Recently, a veteran teacher noted at a conference that she was teaching a multi-age class for the first time in her twenty-plus-year career as an educator. "That must be quite an adjustment for you," said the younger educator seated beside her. The more senior teacher reflected for just a moment and responded, "Actually, it really hasn't been an adjustment for me. I've taught a multi-age classroom every year. But this is just the first time someone put the sign on my door."

What we now call *differentiated instruction* is not new. It simply asks educators to recognize what teachers have known for centuries: students do not arrive at school as "matched sets." Because the pace of brain development varies among children, it is likely that in any third-grade class, some students are reading much like first-graders and others like sixth-graders. A third-grader who reads like a second-grader may be ready to do fractions in mathematics well before most of her classmates. In other words, the fact that all students in a particular classroom share a similar date of birth is no indication that they all learn at the same rate, in the same way, and with the same support systems.

Few educators seriously debate whether a particular chronological age is a trustworthy predictor of a student's academic accomplishments. Most of us who have taught have ample evidence that academic variance is a given among students of any grade level—preschool through graduate school. The fundamental question each teacher has to answer is whether to respond to those differences—and if so, in what way.

A Case in Point

It was just the first week of school, and already Mrs. Worrell felt tired. Her class enrollment was higher this year than last. The students in front of her came from several different language groups, from a broad spectrum of economic groups, and with a five-year span of achievement in reading and math. Her job was to get all of the students ready to pass the same test on the same day under the same conditions. She had nine months to do that. The year stretched ahead of her like a bad movie. She had too many students, virtually no planning time, no one to help in the classroom, a single textbook for each subject, too few supplies, too much content—and a mandate to make sure that everyone would look competent on the test that loomed ahead of them all. She looked at the students as they left the room to get on the afternoon school buses. The students looked as weary as she felt. She wondered if everyone in the building felt that way.

A great number of teachers plan and teach as though all the students in a given classroom were essentially alike. When it becomes evident that some students are confused, lost, or bored, some teachers quickly try to offer additional encouragement, support, or work as a means of addressing the mismatch between lesson and learner. Others simply follow their initial instructional plans. After all, there's a lot of material to cover.

Teaching With a Focus on Learners

Differentiation stems from the research-based perspective that students will engage more fully with learning and will learn more robustly when teachers proactively plan with their differences—as well as their similarities—in mind (Tomlinson et al., 2003). Such an instructional model is learner centered in that it accepts the premise that a teacher's role is not simply to cover material or to expose students to content, but rather to maximize student learning. Therefore, if a student is missing knowledge or skills from the past that are necessary for success with current learning expectations, the teacher's role is to help that student move both backward and forward with essential content. If a student already knows what a teacher is about to teach, the teacher's role is to help that student move beyond current learning expectations so that growth will continue. Similarly, differentiation operates from the premise that if a student cannot learn efficiently or effectively in one mode, a strong teacher looks for another learning mode that will work for that student, and if content seems irrelevant to or disconnected from a student's world, the teacher seeks to build bridges between critical content and student interests.

The bedrock of differentiation is a four-part argument that is foundational to effective teaching:

1. The environment in which students are asked to learn must invite learning. That is, it must be safe, challenging, and supportive for each student.

2. A teacher should be able to clearly delineate what constitutes essential knowledge, understanding, and skills in a content area, unit, and lesson.

3. The teacher should persistently assess student proximity to the essential knowledge, understanding, and skills throughout a segment of study.

4. When ongoing assessment data indicate that a student is confused about, has learning gaps in, or has mastered essential knowledge, understanding, or skills, the teacher should use that information to plan upcoming instruction. The idea is to address those needs—whether for remediation or acceleration—that, if unattended to, will most likely impede student growth.

When we look at differentiation in these terms, we see that it is neither revolutionary nor something extra. It is simply teaching mindfully and with the intent to support the success of each human being for whom we accept professional responsibility. It moves us away from seeing and teaching students as a unit toward reflecting on and responding to them as individuals.

> Differentiation is neither revolutionary nor something extra. It is simply teaching mindfully and with the intent to support the success of each human being for whom we accept professional responsibility.

Differentiation, therefore, is not a particular set of strategies, but a way of thinking about teaching and learning. It provides a framework for planning and carrying out instruction. While a substantial model of differentiation will offer instructional tools and strategies that facilitate attention to varied learner needs, it will also counsel teachers to use those approaches that work for their particular students, for their specific content, and for their strengths and proclivities as professionals.

A Model for Effective Differentiation

Figure 1.1 (page 10) presents one model of differentiation (Tomlinson, 1999, 2001, 2003). Its key components, which we regard as the "nonnegotiables" of effective differentiation, will serve as the foundation for this book. The components are nonnegotiable in the sense that they stem from what we know about how people learn and how strong teachers teach. Each element of the model is part of an interdependent system of classroom elements, and thus when any one of them is weak, the other elements in the system will suffer. Classrooms in which all of the elements work effectively together are classrooms that are likely to work for a broad range of learners. The remainder of this chapter will briefly explain the nonnegotiables and the general support for them in brain research. The rest of the book will explore the nonnegotiables and the brain research that relates to them in greater detail.

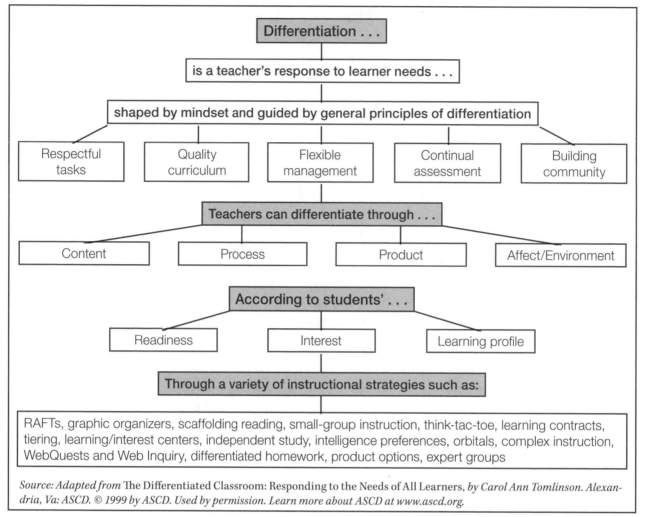

Figure 1.1: A model of differentiation.

The model begins with the assertion that differentiation is a teacher's response to learner needs. We are well aware that teachers these days are very concerned about the impact of state or provincial curriculum standards, Advanced Placement or International Baccalaureate course requirements, and high-stakes testing on their instructional decisions and time. They worry about how they can address these concerns and still respond to the needs of diverse learners through differentiation. Many of the suggestions we will offer do not require much *additional* time in planning and preparation because they should often replace rather than add to current instructional practices.

Further, the model asserts that a teacher's belief about the capacity of each student to succeed with essential content affects everything in the classroom. Teachers who believe that some students are smart and some are not have little difficulty with the outcome when some students succeed academically and others do not. After all, they conclude, that's just the way the world works. By contrast, teachers who believe that virtually all students can master important content as long as they are willing to work hard enough and are supported by a teacher who is willing to work hard enough to lead them to success draw a different conclusion. For those teachers, success is really the only acceptable outcome. Carol Dweck (2006) calls the first perspective a "fixed mindset" and the second a "fluid" or "growth mindset." Teachers with a growth mindset believe it is their role to do what is necessary to be a catalyst for student success and also to enlist the student effort necessary for success. Differentiation calls on teachers to develop a growth mindset and to ensure that their students do so as well. Teacher mindsets will be discussed at length in chapter 2.

The model delineates five key principles that guide effective differentiation. These principles are integral to a classroom system in which all of the parts work together to create peak learning, and they align with the core tenets of differentiation that each student is worthy of dignity and respect and that each student should have access to the best learning opportunities a school can offer.

1. Work in a differentiated classroom is respectful of each student. When students examine the tasks assigned to their peers, they see that every student's work is equally engaging. In addition, the tasks signal that each student is working with the knowledge, understanding, and skills designated as essential for a topic, unit, or lesson and that every student is required to use those essentials in ways that require complex thought and problem solving.

2. Curriculum, or what students will be asked to learn, is rooted in the critical ideas of a topic or discipline. It is designed to support student understanding rather than only recall. Goals for each step of the teaching/learning process are absolutely clear to students and teachers alike. The curriculum itself reflects the teacher's belief that everyone in the class is "smart."

3. Teachers regularly use flexible grouping. Just as they plan the sequence of ideas necessary for learning, they plan a variety of grouping configurations for each stage in the learning process. Groups based on readiness (see chapter 5) can bring together students with similar levels of readiness or mixed levels of readiness. Those based on interest (see chapter 6) can have students working with peers whose interests are like their own or peers whose interests differ from theirs. Groups based on learning preferences (see chapter 7) can bring together students with similar learning preferences or students who learn in different ways. On some occasions, the teacher selects the members of a group. On other occasions, students select their working partners. At still other times, groupings are random. Group sizes vary, as do group names or designations and areas of the room in which a particular group of students will work. These groupings, of course, weave in and out of whole-class instruction. Flexible

grouping enables a teacher to target students' particular learning needs while observing students in a wide range of settings. Students also get to see one another and themselves in varied contexts. In classrooms where flexible grouping is standard practice, students become more aware of their own strengths and those of their peers.

4. Teachers use ongoing assessment to inform their instruction. Being clear at each stage of the learning process about what students should know, understand, and be able to do as a result of that segment, teachers use preassessment of student readiness, interest, and learning profile to understand where students are relative to essential goals as a unit begins. This allows the teacher to "match" instruction to student needs from the outset, including attending to gaps in prerequisite knowledge. Throughout a unit of study, the teacher persistently uses formative assessment to understand who is progressing as he or she should be, who is confused or falling behind, and who is ready to move beyond the fundamental expectations for achievement. Using this continual and unfolding sense of each student's relationship to critical outcomes, the teacher modifies instructional plans to attend to students' varied strengths and needs with the goal of helping each student grow academically as effectively and efficiently as possible (see chapter 4).

5. The learning environment supports students in taking the risk of learning. A positive environment attends to students' affective needs for acceptance, respect, affiliation, contribution, challenge, and support (see chapter 2). Such an environment is neither accidental nor coincidental to learning. It begins with a sensitive, empathetic teacher who values the worth of each learner. It proceeds with the teacher's gradual and intentional connection with every individual student, expands as individuals learn to trust that the teacher is their partner in success, and ultimately connects the students in a teamlike community of mutual regard and support. In such environments, students compete against themselves rather than against one another, and they work together to enhance one another's prospects for success. The learning environment necessary for effective differentiation—and, in fact, for meaning-focused learning—must be both orderly and flexible. Its routines and procedures exist not to "control" students, but to facilitate learning in ways that work best for the various individuals in the class.

The model of differentiation highlights four classroom elements that teachers can modify in response to three categories of student need. Teachers can modify *content* (what students will learn or how they will gain access to what they are asked to learn), *process* (activities through which students make sense of or "come to own" essential content), *product* (how students demonstrate what they know, understand, and can do after extended periods of learning), and *affect* (attention to students' feelings and emotional needs). Modifying these four elements "makes room" for student variance in readiness (proximity to learning goals), interests (proclivities for particular ideas, topics, or skills) and learning profile (preferences for approaches to or modes of learning). As teachers become more competent and confident in adapting content, process, product, and affect in response to student readiness, interest, and learning profile, the likelihood of academic success and maximum student achievement grows exponentially.

Finally, the model presents a variety of instructional strategies that enable teachers to make room for student variance. These are approaches that extend the capacity of the teacher to reach out to students differently when that is warranted yet still keep all learners focused on essential outcomes. Such strategies include small-group instruction, varying materials, learning contracts, tiering, complex instruction, expert groups, jigsaw, and many, many other methods. When teachers are comfortable with a wide range of instructional strategies, addressing students' varied readiness levels, interests, and learning preferences is easier—just as building a house or a piece of furniture is easier with the right tools at hand.

Brain Research Supports Differentiation

We noted earlier that some recent discoveries regarding how the brain learns substantially support the components of differentiation. Although we will discuss these discoveries more thoroughly in the ensuing chapters, here is a brief introduction to seven basic principles about how we learn. Each of these principles is evident in the model of differentiation we use in this book—and in classrooms whose teachers are attuned and responsive to the inevitable diversity among today's students.

1. Each brain is uniquely organized. Even identical twins raised in the same environment view their world differently from each other as a result of their unique experiences and interpretations of how their world works. Although there are basic similarities in how we all learn, there are also important differences. We have individual preferences for how we learn, such as whether we prefer to learn alone or in groups or to learn by listening or by observing or by participating, just to mention a few. These preferences constitute what may be called our own "learning profile." Thus, the pervasive notion that one curricular, instructional, and assessment program fits all is hardly brain-compatible.

2. The brain is a lean pattern-making machine. One of the jobs of the brain's frontal lobe—located just behind the forehead—is to determine whether incoming information has meaning for the individual.

The frontal lobe does this mainly by looking for patterns. The more information the learner can acquire, the more likely that meaningful patterns will soon evolve. The brain is more apt to retain information that has meaning in long-term memory.

3. The brain's frontal lobe is often referred to as the "executive center" because it directs much of the brain's activity. Its responsibilities include processing higher-order thinking and solving problems. The process of *convergent thinking* brings together information to solve a problem that generally has a single correct solution—as, for instance, most tasks in school and answers on tests. Few patterns result from this process. *Divergent thinking*, on the other hand, is a thought process that generates creative ideas by exploring different ways of solving problems. This process often leads to new ideas and concepts, producing novel patterns and expanding existing cognitive networks. Through differentiation, teachers can explore ways to help students become successful divergent thinkers.

4. Emotions are processed in the brain's limbic system and play an important role in pattern making. When information and patterns produce an emotional "Aha!" chemicals are released that stimulate the brain's reward system and keep us motivated to continue learning. However, racing through an overpacked curriculum in a classroom devoid of positive emotions in order to take a high-stakes test raises anxiety and releases chemicals that shut down the brain's higher-order processing. The learner's brain shifts from thinking, "This stuff is interesting," to "How will I ever pass that test?" Tension is high, retention of learning is low. Differentiation offers students more rewarding learning opportunities.

5. Learning is as much a social process as it is a cognitive one. Starting from childhood, we learn by observing others, most likely through the mechanism of our mirror neurons. These clusters of neurons fire not only when we experience a task or an emotion, but also when we see someone else experience the same task or emotion. Students' learning is shaped, too, by the practices and values of the groups to which they belong. How much students participate in class activities, for instance, is often driven by how they think their peers will react if they give an incorrect answer. Self-concept plays a strong role in learning because most individuals tend to avoid situations that may result in failure. Constructive social interactions generate positive emotions and develop executive functions, thereby enhancing learning and retention. Differentiation helps to ensure that constructive environment.

6. We are learning a lot more about our memory systems. Why do students forget so much of what they have been taught? Apparently, we can carry information in working memory (a temporary memory where we do conscious processing) for an extended period of time. The information will eventually fade away if there is no meaningful reason for it to be retained in long-term memory. Could this explain why students can pass a test on a topic today but barely remember it three months later? Differentiation can include instructional strategies that are more likely to result in students' remembering rather than discarding what they learn.

7. Learning for retention requires focus and extended attention. Students today have many demands on their attention, much of them from new and exciting forms of technology. Because the brain is constantly searching for meaning, students will give their attention to what they find personally meaningful. And the more meaningful it is, the more engaged they will become. When students perceive a learning objective as lacking meaning, for whatever reason, their attention is likely to divert to more stimulating—and off-task—activities. Differentiation can tailor activities to meet individual student needs, thereby maintaining student interest and focus.

All of these insights into the learning process reaffirm how important it is for teachers to recognize individual student needs; to differentiate their curriculum content, instructional approaches, and assessments; and to provide rich, stimulating, brain-friendly, and productive classroom environments. We know more now, and we should adjust our educational practices accordingly.

Differentiation in a Nutshell

Effective differentiation does not call on a teacher to be all things to every student at all times of the day. Rather, it calls on teachers to be consistently mindful of three things: (1) how their content is structured for meaning and authenticity, (2) who their students are as individuals, and (3) which elements in their classrooms give them degrees of freedom in connecting content and learners. It is our belief that this approach to teaching has long been supported by classroom practice and by research on pedagogy. We also believe that our new and growing understanding of how the brain develops and learns contributes to the case for quality differentiation.

A Better Scenario

Mrs. Worrell looked at the students as they left her room at the end of the first week of school. She knew that some of the students couldn't wait to leave the room and that others would happily stay on for a longer day. She knew that some of the students had understood the ideas they explored that day, that others had not, and that some had known the content before she began teaching it to them. She knew that their lives at home ran the gamut from comfortable and supportive to overly demanding to chaotic to abusive. She knew that some of the students flourished when they worked with peers and that others preferred working alone—or had no one they could call a friend.

In those children, she saw herself as a young learner—shy, uncertain, and eager to please. She saw her son, who often learned faster than his agemates and who got weary of waiting for others to learn what he already knew. She saw her daughter, who often needed extra time to learn and who learned best when someone could show her how something worked rather than simply tell her. She knew she needed to create a classroom where there was room for each student to succeed. She wasn't sure exactly how to do that, but she had some good hunches and the determination to follow them. She was excited to see a new school week begin.

CHAPTER 2

Mindset, Learning Environment, and Differentiation

All good teachers will tell you that the most important quality they bring to their teaching is their love for the children. But what does that mean? It means that before we can teach them, we need to delight in them. Someone once said that children need one thing in order to succeed in life: someone who is crazy about them. We need to find a way to delight in all our students. We may be the only one in their lives to do so. We need to look for the best, expect the best, find something in each child that we can truly treasure. . . . If children recognize that we have seen their genius, who they really are, they will have the confidence and resilience to take risks in learning. I am convinced that many learning and social difficulties would disappear if we learned to see the genius in each child and then created a learning environment that encourages it to develop.

—Steven Levy, *Starting From Scratch: One Classroom Builds Its Own Curriculum*

Hopefully, most teachers have had those days or moments of sheer professional joy when something clicks in the classroom or for a particular student and it is, at least for a time, undeniable that teaching can possess and be possessed by magic. No doubt most teachers have also had their share of moments during which the mountain that is teaching seems too high to climb. Both of these are outlier moments—the former leading us to conclude that all of our students are brilliant and the latter, that they are all beyond our reach.

In less manic or depressive moments, our reactions to students are shaped by attitudes that have evolved unconsciously and over time. Some of us, for instance, are drawn to students who are quiet and compliant, while others gravitate to the student who is full of surprises and challenges. Some of us may work more easily with boys, while others find it easier to work with girls. Sometimes teachers have difficulty seeing the world through the eyes of students who have come to school from economic backgrounds or cultures that differ markedly from their own. These sorts of preferences or limitations can certainly bear on teaching effectiveness. The more aware we are of such feelings, the more likely we are to deal with them in productive ways. If our attitudes, beliefs, or mindsets about teaching, learning, and our students go unexamined, the consequences can be pernicious for some or many of the young people we teach.

A Case in Point

Carlos feels invisible in class. Ms. Atcheson is polite to him, but she evidently does not expect much from him in the way of grades and achievement. When he fails to do his homework, she reminds him it will hurt his grade, but she does not seem surprised that the assignment is missing. She never calls on him in class discussions, and most of the work she assigns him looks like baby work to him. Carlos has never been a good student, so her response to him is familiar. He is just as happy staying in the background.

Liza is another story. Clearly, Ms. Atcheson thinks she is smart. Ms. Atcheson often comments to the class on her work and calls on her and three or four other kids more than everyone else put together. The one time Liza did not have her homework, Ms. Atcheson seemed stunned and told Liza she was disappointed. Liza has mixed feelings about the class. On the one hand, it's good to know that the teacher likes you and thinks you are smart. On the other hand, Liza feels a little dishonest. She sees the students around her working hard and nearly always getting lower grades than she does. It does not take much for her to make As. That doesn't seem quite right.

What Are Mindsets?

Mindsets are the assumptions, expectations, and beliefs that guide our behavior and our interactions with others. These mindsets start forming at an early age. As we grow and interact with our parents, friends, and elements of our culture, we store summaries of those interactions in our brain. Our brain's frontal lobe, where cognitive processing is carried out, reviews these summaries regularly and coordinates with the emotional (limbic) areas to determine how we should respond to similar interactions in the future. Over time, these summaries get stored in cerebral networks. New experiences strengthen and expand these networks. Eventually, the networks become so ingrained that we react almost reflexively when similar situations do arise. For example, when we spot a dear friend, neural circuits fire in the emotional and motor areas of the brain, causing us to spontaneously smile, extend our arms, and show warmth when we meet. On the other hand, different circuits might fire in the presence of a demanding boss, causing us to stiffen and display deference.

We develop mindsets about many things. To name a few, we have mindsets about religion, politics, our jobs, our futures, each of our family members, and anybody we interact with regularly. Because mindsets in adults are so well established in neural networks, they are difficult to change. For example, media coverage of news events can lead to stereotyping of people of color or of women. Constantly viewing these stereotypes makes them difficult to overcome. Moreover, research in neuroscience has found that the neural networking of mindsets is very complex (Mitchell, Banaji, & Macrae, 2005). It may take much more neural effort to change one part of a mindset network than to change the entire network (Diamond, 2009). These findings would imply that high motivation and considerable persistence are needed to change a mindset, but it can be done.

Mindsets are the assumptions, expectations, and beliefs that guide our behavior and our interactions with others.

Teachers have mindsets about their jobs, colleagues, and students. They may not even be aware of some of the assumptions and beliefs they hold in their mindsets, yet these attitudes can still affect their behavior and be communicated to others. Have you ever discussed a student's work and behavior with another teacher who had the same student and felt like you were talking about two different people? Why did that happen? Most likely, you and the other teacher were looking at this student with very different mindsets. Here's an example: picture a student who is constantly raising questions during a lesson. One teacher may get angry at this student without realizing that the anger stems from the assumption that the student's persistent asking of questions is an attempt to derail the lesson. In contrast, another teacher may interpret the student's questions as an honest effort to thoroughly understand the lesson's content. The teachers' mindsets result in different interpretations of the student's behavior and, consequently, in different teacher responses.

The Effective Teacher's Mindset

Brooks and Goldstein (2008) suggest that effective teachers have a characteristic mindset that guides their behavior throughout the teaching and learning processes. As we will show in the following discussion, many of the assumptions and beliefs that make up that mindset are particularly pertinent to the learning environment in differentiated classrooms.

Teachers Have a Lifelong Impact

Those of us who have taught realize that we can influence our students' lives for years to come. The research literature on child resilience highlights the extent of our impact. It shows that several factors enable children of misfortune to beat the heavy odds against them. One factor is the presence in their lives of a charismatic adult—a person with whom they can identify and from whom they gather strength. In a surprising number of cases, that person turns out to be a teacher. Thus, effective teachers recognize that they are in a unique position to be charismatic adults in students' lives.

One of the authors remembers working years ago with a high school sophomore who wanted to go to college but had little confidence in his academic abilities. The author provided continuing encouragement and extra help for the student during his junior and senior years. Having gained self-confidence, the student went on to graduate from the U.S. Air Force Academy. While flying combat missions over Kuwait during Operation Desert Storm, the student—now an Air Force major—sent a note to the author expressing thanks for encouraging him during his difficult days in high school.

Even small gestures—such as a warm greeting, a note of encouragement, taking a few minutes to meet alone with a student, and showing an appreciation of and respect for different learning needs in a differentiated classroom—can have a lifelong impact.

The Classroom Must Feel Safe and Secure

The foundation for successful learning and for a safe and secure classroom climate is the relationship that teachers develop with their students. Why is this so significant? To answer this question, we need to briefly explain how the brain handles incoming information. Figure 2.1 illustrates the hierarchy of response to sensory input. It is important to understand that any input that is of higher priority diminishes the processing of lower-priority data.

The brain's main job is to help its owner survive. Thus, data interpreted as posing a threat to the survival of the individual, such as a burning odor, a snarling dog, or someone threatening bodily injury, are processed immediately. When the stimulus is received, a rush of adrenaline is sent throughout the brain. This *reflexive* response shuts down all unnecessary activity and directs the brain's attention to the source of the stimulus.

Emotional data also take high priority. When an individual responds emotionally to a situation, the limbic system takes command, and complex cognitive processes are suspended. We have all had experiences when anger, fear of the unknown, or joy quickly overcame our rational thoughts. Under certain conditions, emotions can enhance memory by causing the release of hormones that signal brain regions to strengthen memory. In other words, strong emotions can simultaneously shut down conscious processing during an event and enhance our memory of it. Emotion is a powerful and misunderstood force in learning and memory.

The brain's reaction to both survival stimuli and powerful emotions is reflexive, that is, it occurs instinctively and without prior planning. If neither threats to survival nor strong emotions are present, the brain can turn its attention to processing factual information and concepts. This is a *reflective* process that allows learning to take place by making connections to previous experiences and by building cognitive networks.

Students must feel physically safe and emotionally secure before they can focus on the curriculum.

Another way of stating the hierarchy illustrated in figure 2.1 is that before students will turn their attention to cognitive learning (the curriculum), they must feel physically safe and emotionally secure.

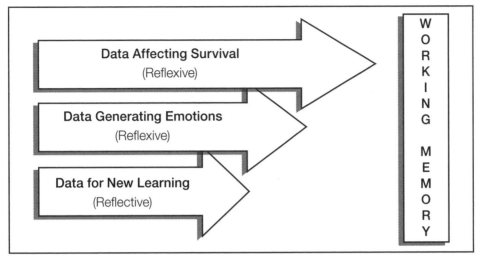

Figure 2.1: The hierarchy of response to sensory input.

All Students Want to Succeed

The belief that students want to succeed is related to the growth mindset we will discuss later in this chapter. The human brain does not deal well with failure. If a student is not learning, the teacher must determine how to modify his or her teaching style and instructional material to meet that student's needs. If a teacher believes that certain students are inherently lazy or unmotivated, then that negative mindset leads the teacher to respond to these students with annoyance. That response sets the stage for a negative learning environment and alters the emotional state of the students.

Figure 2.2 (page 22) illustrates how positive and negative learning environments affect body chemistry, thereby altering the emotions and learning of those in the classroom. In positive learning climates, chemicals called *endorphins* are running through the bloodstream. These are the body's natural painkillers and mood elevators. They produce a sense of euphoria, so that an individual feels good about being in the situation. They raise the pain threshold, so minor aches are no longer bothersome. Most importantly, they stimulate the frontal lobe to remember the situation and whatever it is processing at the moment—most likely the learning objective.

However, in a negative learning environment, very different biochemical reactions are at work. Negative climates create stress, which causes the hormone *cortisol* to enter the bloodstream. This chemical is a powerful steroid that raises an individual's anxiety level. It also prompts the frontal lobe to stop processing low-priority information, such as the learning objective, in order to focus on the cause of the stress and decide how to reduce or remove it. Thus, the frontal lobe remembers the situation, but the learning objective has already dropped out of the memory systems.

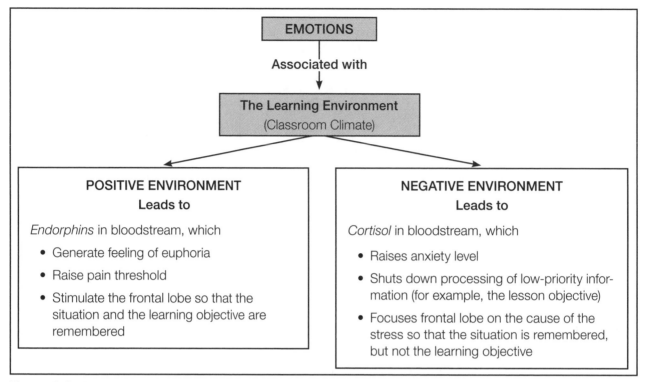

Figure 2.2: The impact of the learning environment on body chemistry.

Teachers who believe that all students come to school desiring to learn will figure out different ways to reach and teach them when they are uninterested or frustrated. This positive mindset has a profound impact on the ways that teachers respond in the classroom, especially to those students who are struggling. When students lose faith in their ability to learn, they often turn to counterproductive ways of coping, such as misbehaving or withdrawing. This situation is less likely to occur in a differentiated classroom, where students of varying abilities have a better chance of success and where teachers' negative assumptions are far less apt to prevail.

The Social-Emotional Needs of Students Must Be Met

Attending to the social-emotional needs of students is not a digression that draws time away from teaching academic subjects but rather is an important part of classroom practice. Students are not just learning the curriculum; they are learning about themselves, how they interact with their peers, and how they choose their friends. They are also learning to deal with their emotions, such as how they react to failure and how they respond to the opposite sex.

In recent years, a new field of study called *social cognitive neuroscience* has emerged. Brain-imaging technology has allowed researchers in this field to answer a long-standing question: are the cerebral mechanisms and neural networks involved in the processing of social stimuli (for example, forming relationships, comparing others to oneself, or interpreting the behavior of others) different from those involved in the processing of nonsocial stimuli (for example, dealing with hunger and sleep)? Apparently, the answer is yes. Studies now indicate that specific brain regions are activated when subjects are faced with making social decisions and judgments as part of a performance task (Mitchell et al., 2005; Olson, Plotzker, & Ezzyat, 2007).

The neural networks that process social stimuli are different from those that process nonsocial stimuli.

One surprising finding was the discovery of spindle-shaped neurons in the front part of the brain. These neurons are larger and have fewer branches than the neurons typically found in brain tissue. Called *von Economo neurons*, after the man who first described them, they are found only in human beings, great apes, and a few other distinctly gregarious animals. Researchers note that the von Economo neurons are found in similar places in the brains of these animals and speculate that they play a major role in generating social emotions and monitoring social interactions. Figure 2.3 shows the location of the two sites where von Economo neurons are found in humans, the *anterior cingulate cortex* and the *frontal insula* (Chen, 2009).

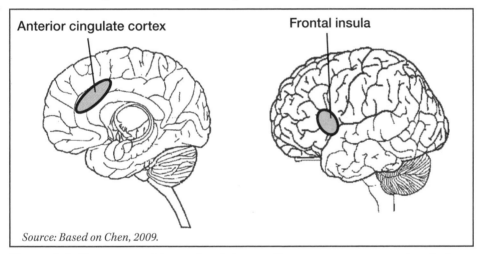

Source: Based on Chen, 2009.

Figure 2.3: Two areas of the brain where von Economo neurons are located.

Additional evidence that the von Economo neurons are associated with social interactions comes from studies of people who have a degenerative disease called *frontotemporal dementia*. These patients lose their social graces, show no empathy, and turn irresponsible, erratic, and insensitive. In one study, brain imaging revealed that the dementia had targeted the neurons in the anterior cingulate cortex and frontal insula (Brambati et al., 2007).

Having brain regions and neurons dedicated to processing social interactions suggests how important social relationships are to human development and behavior. In the brain of children and adolescents, the frontal lobe is not mature enough to exert complete control over social and emotional processing. As a result, social and emotional needs are a high priority with many students (Sousa, 2009). Of course, a high percentage of the social interactions in schools occur between teachers and students. During a school day, many students spend more time with all of their teachers than with any of their parents, siblings, or peers. This reality alone makes it crucial for the student and the teacher to perceive, assess, and respond to each other's behavior accurately and adequately. Effective teachers recognize these needs and find ways to address them while still managing to present the curriculum objectives.

Empathy Is Very Important

For teacher-student relationships to be effective, teachers must be empathetic and attempt to perceive the world through their students' eyes. Researchers have discovered that students who have caring relationships with their teachers perform better academically than students who do not. Furthermore, empathy can potentially foster openness, attentiveness, and positive relationships, especially in culturally diverse classrooms. Being open and flexible helps teachers adjust to varying contexts and improves their ability to differentiate instruction and curriculum to fit their students' needs (Gay, 2000; McAllister & Irvine, 2002).

Empathetic teachers ask themselves if they would want someone to say or do to them what they have just said or done to a student, colleague, or parent. For instance, teachers sometimes try to motivate underperforming students by urging them to "try harder." Although the remark may be well intentioned, the teacher is assuming that the students are unwilling to expend the time and energy necessary to succeed. Consequently, students frequently construe this comment to be accusatory and judgmental. When students feel accused, they are less apt to be cooperative. The teacher's comment fails to lead to the desired results, which, in turn, may further reinforce the teacher's belief that the students are unmotivated.

Students Should Feel a Sense of Ownership of Their Education

Teachers who believe that students should feel ownership of their education and success welcome frequent student input. Whenever students feel their voice is being heard, they tend to work cooperatively with teachers and are more motivated to meet their academic challenges (Carroll et al., 2009; McQuillan, 2005). Furthermore, having a voice reinforces their feelings of personal control and responsibility, which are essential ingredients of a positive school climate. One good way to give students a sense of ownership is to ask them to consider what rules are needed in the classroom for all students to feel comfortable and learn best.

Teachers Should Identify and Reinforce Each Student's Areas of Competence

Too often we focus on our students' problems and vulnerabilities and afford little time to reinforcing their strengths and competencies. One obvious strategy for helping students feel competent is to teach them in the ways in which they can learn best. Because each student has different learning needs and strengths, teachers should familiarize themselves with such topics as multiple intelligences, learning style characteristics, and gender- and culture-influenced learning preferences. We will discuss each of these topics in detail in chapter 7 and will consider their implications for differentiating instruction.

Another strategy for enhancing a sense of competence is to offer students opportunities to help others. For example, older students with learning problems could read to younger children, or students of varying abilities could work together as a team, bringing their own unique strengths to different projects. Students experience more positive feelings toward school and are more motivated to learn if they are encouraged to contribute to the school environment.

Teachers Should Address Fears of Failure and Humiliation

As mentioned earlier, fear is an intense emotional response that shuts down higher cognitive processes so that the brain can focus on the source of the fear and decide how to deal with it. Deciding how to manage fear is the responsibility of the brain's frontal lobe. In children and adolescents, the frontal lobe is not fully developed, so it has limited ability to interpret and dampen the fear response.

One of the greatest obstacles to learning is the fear of making mistakes. Because many students equate making mistakes with feeling humiliated, they will avoid learning tasks that appear too challenging. Effective teachers know that to prevent this situation, it is best to openly address these fears with students. One technique for lessening students' fear of failure is for teachers to share stories from their own school days about being afraid of or actually making mistakes, such as failing a test. Their openness may invite students to share some of their thoughts and feelings about making mistakes. Teachers can ask what they can do and what the students can do as a class to minimize the fear of failure.

By sharing their own experiences of making mistakes, teachers can help lower students' fear of failure.

Discipline Is a Teaching Process

Discipline is a process for teaching acceptable behaviors rather than a process of intimidation and humiliation. Classes with well-planned, engaging lessons rarely have discipline problems, because students feel successful while taking part in meaningful learning experiences. Their cerebral reward circuits are activated, and distracting behaviors are avoided. When a behavior problem does arise, teachers who believe discipline is a way of teaching remind the student of the appropriate behavior and attempt later to determine the cause of the misbehavior. The emphasis is always on what the student *did* and not who the student *is,* and on understanding and addressing the reasons for the misbehavior rather than "punishing" it.

In these classrooms, teachers start every day with the expectation that students will behave appropriately. They have a few rules that all students clearly understand. They enforce the rules consistently, act fairly, deal with discipline problems immediately and with the least amount of interruption, avoid confrontations in front of students, and know how to use humor (not sarcasm) to defuse tense situations. See chapter 8 for specific suggestions on managing the differentiated classroom.

Fixed and Growth Mindsets

Carol Dweck has spent much of her career examining people's mindsets about learning—about what it means to be smart and how success happens. Her work is profoundly important for educators, reminding us that our preconceptions shape our beliefs and our actions—as well as the beliefs and actions of the students we teach. These ideas are particularly significant for the teaching philosophy of differentiation. Dweck (2006) finds through decades of research that we develop at a young age either a fixed or a fluid mindset about the origins of ability and success. Those who develop a fixed mindset accept the premise that we are born smart or not smart—able or not able—in a particular domain. In this line of thinking, environments can contribute to our "smart quotient" or prospects for success, but the genetic predisposition to be a good mathematician or a poor one, a great soccer player or a mediocre one, is so strong that it will win the day in determining the likelihood that an individual will do well in a given pursuit.

By contrast, people who develop a fluid or growth mindset operate from a radically different perspective on ability and success. Growth-mindset individuals believe that while genetics might sketch out a starting point in our development, one's own determination and persistence—in combination with persistent and determined support—are really what predict success. Most likely, few teachers are aware of fixed- and fluid-mindset options or have had occasion to unpack and examine their own perspectives on student ability and success. Nonetheless, our practice and our students are shaped by where we stand. Certainly, teacher success with differentiation is framed by mindset.

Mindset, Teaching, and Learning

Teachers with fixed mindsets, consciously or unconsciously, accept the premise that some students will learn and some will not, largely because of their genetics and home environments. Such teachers set out to determine who is smart or capable and who is not. From that point, it seems to make good sense to separate students by their perceived ability and to teach them accordingly. Teachers with a fixed mindset often have bluebird-buzzard type groups in the classroom, making it evident to virtually everyone whom they perceive to be "smart" and whom they perceive to be "not smart." Sometimes they opt to form whole classes of "smart" kids and corresponding classes of "not smart" kids. In either case, they then accept the logic of accelerating the smart kids and remediating the others. They teach some students at high levels of Bloom's Taxonomy and others at low levels, pleased to have a framework that *seems* well suited to the various locations of students on the chain of ability. A fixed mindset also disposes these teachers to like labels that seem to explain what problems hinder some students and what advantages propel others.

By contrast, teachers with fluid mindsets begin with the premise that most students can learn most things if they exert the effort necessary to do so. They also accept the related premise that the teacher's role is to elicit that effort and to join with the student in doing whatever it takes to succeed. They "teach up"—that is, they create work designed to stretch a student and then partner with that student to ensure that he or she has the support and scaffolding necessary to master what initially seemed out of reach. Teachers with fluid mindsets want to see students in a variety of classroom groupings—no bluebirds and buzzards, but rather students functioning in an array of contexts that yield insight about what works for them. These teachers have little use for labels but rather seek understanding of what to do tomorrow to help students move to the next step in learning. They neither accept excuses about why a student can't learn or hasn't completed work nor buy into the notion that advanced learners should receive high grades for work that was too easy for them. They are proponents of a staunch work ethic for everyone—themselves included.

Teachers, of course, signal to students their conclusions about the likelihood of their success. It is not surprising to hear that students who know they are seen as "not smart" come to see themselves as not smart and students who know they are seen as smart come to see themselves that way as well. Of greater significance, however, is that the "not smart" students attribute their lack of success to factors beyond their control, making statements such as "Nobody in my family is good at math," or "I just don't have any talent as a singer." Often, students who hold such beliefs give up in the face of difficulty because they believe the ability to do the work is simply not in them.

Ironically, when teachers put a premium on being smart rather than on working hard, highly able students suffer as well. They conclude that smart is something they were born with. When they encounter work they cannot easily accomplish, it seems to indicate that they are not smart after all, because smart people do not have to work hard, and this task would require serious work. Often, then, such students will reject the challenge. In fact, bright students with a fixed mindset often select easier tasks within a class, opt to take easier classes, reject feedback on their work as negative judgment, and work for grades rather than for the sake of learning, because it is the grade that signals success and smartness.

In contrast, students working with teachers who insist that everyone can succeed if he or she works hard enough and that effort, not genetics, is what should be celebrated come to believe that they can have an impact on their own success. They develop a sense of self-efficacy as learners and are more likely than their fixed-mindset peers to learn for the sake of learning, to persist in the face of difficulty, and to see feedback as a mechanism for continued improvement. Students who have previously neither seen themselves as capable and successful nor been seen that way begin to work harder, thus contributing to their own success and to a more efficacious image of themselves. Students who have always seen themselves as smart and therefore as someone who should not have to work hard begin to understand the reality that growth and comfort cannot coexist and that the nearly universal hallmark of great contributors to society is that they worked harder than their peers.

Figure 2.4 describes the learning environments that result from different combinations of student and teacher mindsets. Clearly, developing a fluid or growth mindset is important to both teacher and student success. It is essential to an effectively differentiated classroom.

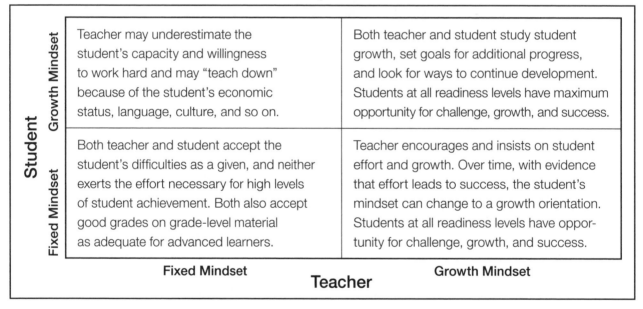

Figure 2.4: Possible combinations of fixed and growth mindsets.

Fixed and Growth Mindsets and Differentiation

There is ample research evidence that people can and do change their mindsets. Teachers in differentiated classrooms need to be particularly cognizant of their beliefs about where ability comes from and what it means to be smart. At the very least, they should strive to develop a growth mindset. The model of differentiation on which this book is based advocates an approach to teaching that is difficult to implement effectively with a fixed mindset. Some principles of the model follow. Think about how a teacher with a fixed mindset versus one with a fluid mindset would respond to the implementation of each of these principles:

- Student openness to the risk of learning begins when a teacher connects with each student and indicates a belief in that student's value and potential.

- The teacher builds community, beginning with modeling his or her respect for the possibilities of each member of the class.

- Each student must have consistent responsibilities for the successful operation of the class.

- Students learn to work with increasing independence and self-awareness as learners.

- Students need to be partners in the belief that every student in the class can and will succeed with the most essential content.

- Fairness is defined as making sure that all students get the support they need to succeed.

- Success is defined, at least in part, as student growth, which means that students compete against themselves rather than against one another.

- The teacher "teaches up"—that is, he or she establishes high expectations and differentiates to support all students in achieving high-level goals.

- The teacher uses flexible grouping practices to "audition" each student in various contexts so that students see themselves in different settings and have a wide range of opportunities to succeed.

- All students work with "respectful tasks"—that is, tasks are differentiated in response to individual students' needs, but all tasks are equally interesting, equally appealing, equally important, and equally dependent on high levels of reasoning.

A teacher with a growth mindset is well positioned to say to students—through actions and words—"I'm so glad you're here. I'm excited to learn about each one of you because I'm convinced that all of you can succeed at a higher level than you had ever thought possible. My job is to work with you to establish a classroom that makes it possible for everyone to succeed. I'm going to ask a great deal of you and also of myself as we work together, because it is your effort and my effort on your behalf that will result in your success. I need your insights about yourself, about one another, and about our class. We will be stronger for the presence of each of you in our classroom." A teacher with a fixed mindset will find such thoughts much less natural and intuitive.

Likewise, the students of the teacher with a growth mindset will receive consistent signals as well as direct guidance and purposeful actions that will lead them to see the connections between their effort and their success at a high level. However, students of a teacher with a fixed mindset will probably find the signals and connections to be far less clear.

Exercise 2.1 (page 36) offers some questions to help teachers think about their own mindsets and the implications of their responses for differentiation. As the chapter continues, it will be helpful to think about links between teacher mindset and the kind of learning environment that can maximize the growth and success of each learner in a classroom that will inevitably be academically diverse.

Classroom Environments and Differentiation

Learning environments are largely invisible yet permeate everything that happens in a classroom. Perhaps because of their invisibility, we tend not to talk about them very much in faculty meetings, staff development sessions, or professional conversations. These missed opportunities diminish teachers' awareness of this critical aspect of schooling and their intentionality in developing environments that actively invite learning.

We can see examples all around us of how environment shapes our responses to events. Most of us have been to a restaurant where the surroundings are appealing, staff members are welcoming, waiters are attentive to our particular tastes, and the food is an art form. Most of us have also been to a different restaurant where the food is equally good, but those who interact with us are too attentive or not attentive enough, where the surroundings are overdone or drab and "greasy," where someone is arguing loudly at the next table, where the service takes far too long, or where we feel we are obliged to swallow dinner whole so that the people waiting nearby can be seated. The same extraordinary food in the latter settings cannot make up for the environmental missteps, and we are unlikely to leave those settings with a desire to invest our resources there again.

Similarly, the medical profession has learned a great deal about the contributions of positive environments to healing. These days, when one walks into a hospital lobby or waiting area, it looks more like a hotel than like the austere hospitals of a generation ago. Even hospital rooms are often painted in pastels, have comfortable chairs for guests, and allow family to stay overnight. Medical personnel now readily share information with patients and solicit their help in decision making. The results are a lessening of patient apprehension and better overall patient attitudes and outcomes.

Classroom environments are no less critical to outcomes for young learners, who typically lack power and autonomy in school settings. In many ways, in fact, classroom environments are harbingers of cognitive and academic outcomes. Just as adults are affected by their environments, students are encouraged or discouraged, energized or deflated, invited or alienated by classroom environments. Positive learning environments prepare students for the difficult task of learning. They open students up to the possibilities of what lies ahead. In that way, learning environments have profound implications for learners both affectively and cognitively.

> Learning environments have profound implications for learners both affectively and cognitively.

Learning Environments, Student Affect, and Differentiation

Many readers may recall that, long ago, Abraham Maslow (1943) proposed that human beings have a hierarchy of needs consisting of five levels. Needs at the more fundamental levels have to be satisfied before needs at the higher levels can be effectively addressed. In the hierarchical progression, physiological or biological requirements such as food, shelter, and sleep are at the first level. Once those needs are addressed, the need for safety and security takes center stage at the second level. The third level is the need for belonging, affection, and love, while esteem and respect (which stem from achievement) are at the fourth level. Only when all these levels of need are met can a person strive to attend to the fifth, and highest, level of need—that of becoming self-actualized, or becoming what one was meant to be.

The implications of Maslow's hierarchy for learning are evident and are further supported by the recent research, discussed earlier, on how the brain prioritizes incoming information (see fig. 2.1, page 21). If young people come to school hungry or sleepy or both, they need a classroom environment in which the teacher is prepared to address those fundamental needs. When those basic survival needs are adequately addressed, students then turn their attention to the need for safety and security.

Feeling safe certainly includes a sense that the school and classroom are protected from intruders, violence, and other forces that, regrettably, are very real in the world of contemporary students. Protection from those sorts of violations is a school-level responsibility. In the classroom, maintaining safety and security includes having structures such as class rules and routines that lend predictability to the day. It extends to the assurance that students do not make fun of one another, belittle one another, or bully one another. Many students at all grade levels come to school each day feeling vulnerable to peers, to society, and even to their families. If the learning environment is crafted to address issues of safety and security, the classroom becomes an oasis of order in an otherwise unreliable world. If the learning environment feels unsafe and insecure, an intangible but very real barrier stands between the student and academic growth. Every student— not just the ones we might identify as vulnerable—needs an abiding sense that the classroom has protective "rules of the road" and that those rules will be universally followed. Such assurance and knowledge provide a stability that allows attention to the next higher level of need.

With adequate attention to safety and security, students seek belonging, affection, and love. Shaped by a fluid or growth mindset, the teacher's positive regard for each student sends initial signals that the classroom has a place for everyone—that everyone is worthy of respect. A teacher who is attuned to students' needs helps the students work collaboratively, celebrate one another's successes, support one another's needs, and create positive memories as the year progresses. In this way, the classroom becomes a community.

Clearly, we do a disservice to teachers (and to their students) when we imply that their job is simply to convey content. If the learning environment confounds student needs at any level of Maslow's hierarchy below achievement, esteem, and respect, that creates barriers to students' academic success. The model of brain-friendly differentiation around which this book is developed counsels teachers that virtually all students enter their classrooms seeking affirmation, contribution, purpose, challenge, and power. Further, the model advises that the most effective teachers respond to those student needs with invitation, investment, opportunity, persistence, and reflection (Tomlinson, 2003). The model reflects the following beliefs:

- Teaching and learning are rooted in a teacher's response to a learner's fundamental needs.

- Students in a given classroom will have common affective needs shared by all human beings.

- Students in a given classroom will inevitably bring varied experiences that have shaped their emotional development and will require personalized affective attention to help them grow from their current points of development.

- Attending to students' affective needs is both a precursor to and an integral part of effective teaching.

> Differentiation advises teachers to respond to student needs with invitation, investment, opportunity, persistence, and reflection.

In other words, learning environments that support academic success for each student proactively address both affective and cognitive needs, and teachers who develop such environments understand the interface between affective and cognitive growth. Exercise 2.2 (page 38) offers some questions to help teachers think about the relationship between student affect, learning environment, and differentiation and to reflect on ways to refine learning environments to benefit student growth.

Learning Environments, Student Cognition, and Differentiation

There was a time long ago when prevailing wisdom suggested that every child was born as a blank slate—a tabula rasa. As adults wrote on those slates, so the theory went, students would learn what they needed to know.

Although that theory has long been discredited, classrooms often still function as though the teacher's job were to tell students what they need to know, and the students' job were to absorb what they hear. Creating a learning environment to support that theory of learning is relatively simple. All that is needed is a room with rows of desks, a teacher who is prepared to tell students what they need to know, and students who learn to sit in the rows of desks and listen quietly to what the teacher has to say.

If psychologists had not already discredited that approach to teaching and learning, simply spending time observing in classrooms would relieve a sentient being of any illusion that the "tell and absorb" approach works. Students in such a setting may (or may not) sit and listen, but they typically do not retain, recall, or transfer what they hear. Neither do they generally become engaged with learning. What we now know about how students learn requires quite a different and more complex learning environment.

Brain-imaging studies are providing increasing evidence that stimulating learning environments may be responsible for more rapid and robust neuron development in children and adolescents. Although genetics certainly play a role in brain growth, many neuroscientists suspect that environmental influences probably play an even greater role (Rao et al., 2010; Shaw et al., 2006). Maintaining a rich learning environment, of course, should be the goal of all schools, but the research implies that school experiences for children and adolescents may have a significant impact on an individual's brain development and eventual level of intelligence. That bears repeating: what happens in classrooms may actually raise or lower a student's IQ!

> Brain studies suggest that a stimulating learning environment may have a significant impact on an individual's brain development and eventual level of intelligence.

Exercise 2.3 (page 41) invites teachers and administrators to reflect on a summary of what we know about learners, the nature of their learning, and the kind of environment necessary to support each student's ability to learn (National Research Council, 1999). Among the qualities that make learning environments conducive to developing student cognition, we know that three are particularly important:

1. Our best knowledge and understanding of the nature of the learning process points to _learner-centered_ classroom environments. That is, teachers teach better when they systematically study their students to increase their understanding of both the age group as a whole and the individuals within that age group. This understanding enables them to focus the content on student needs. Texts, as well as thoughtfully developed content outlines and pacing guides, can be helpful in determining what teachers should emphasize and how much time they should allot to various aspects of the curriculum. Scripted texts may be carefully planned to cover content, but they are poorly suited to addressing the varied learning needs of the students who use them. These common tools should never drive the teaching/learning process.

2. Our best knowledge of how people learn leads to the conclusion that learning environments must be *flexible* in order to maximize students' cognitive development. That is, teachers must be prepared to use time, space, materials, groupings, strategies, and other classroom elements in multiple ways to address students' multiple developmental trajectories. To assume that all students in a particular class will benefit from trying to learn the same thing in the same way over the same time period and with the same support systems rejects what we know about student variance.

3. Our best knowledge of how people learn indicates that environments that serve as catalysts for students' cognitive growth are *rich and stimulating*. That is, the learning environment provides materials, models, and human interactions that tap into and feed students' natural interests, learning preferences, curiosity, and desire for successful autonomy. Because students have different interests, inclinations, strengths, weaknesses, and approaches to learning, instructional resources will necessarily have to be both varied and matched to student needs. Remember that the brain is a strong pattern-seeker. It is continually looking for ways to weave new learning and past learning into a conceptual pattern that makes sense and has meaning. Rich and stimulating environments are the places where such connections, pattern development, and retention of learning can best occur.

Classroom environments with the three qualities just listed are mindfully designed to promote student responsibility, self-awareness as a learner, and learning for the satisfaction of learning. They are not about creating cute bulletin boards or protective cocoons, but rather about building a context that capitalizes on the human inclination to learn in order to achieve one's potential and to contribute to the time and place in which one lives. Exercise 2.4 (page 42) offers some questions to help teachers think about the relationship between student cognition, learning environment, and differentiation and to reflect on ways to refine learning environments to benefit student development.

As you read further in this book about the principles of differentiation and the ways in which our current knowledge of the brain supports and amplifies those principles, it will be helpful to continue to think about the impact of teacher mindset and learning environment on each principle. No sharp line exists between classroom elements; they are both overlapping and interdependent. Strengthening any one of them makes the others more robust, while failure to attend to any of them results in some deterioration of the others.

> Differentiated classroom environments are designed to promote student responsibility, self-awareness as a learner, and learning for the satisfaction of learning.

A Better Scenario

Ms. Atcheson told her students on the first day of class that the two most important things being a teacher had taught her were that every student in her class could be a successful student and that it was her job to make sure that happened. "You all come to class with different strengths and different experiences," she told them, "so you won't learn everything in the same way or at the same time. But each one of you will learn more than you ever thought you could in this class." She told the students the one thing she would insist on was that they come to class every day ready to work as hard as they possibly could. "I promise you I'll come every day to work with you as hard as I can."

"Each day," she said to them, "I'm going to ask each of you to take your next step toward success. It won't necessarily be the same step as the person next to you, but it will be what you need to do in order to grow as a learner that day."

Carlos was suspicious. He had, after all, never been a good student. Liza was worried. She was not sure she knew how to work hard. Both students found the class to be very challenging. Both students "hit a wall" from time to time, but Ms. Atcheson always made sure they had the support to get up and try again. At the end of the year, Carlos said it was the first time he had ever felt smart in school. Liza said this was the first class in which she had ever really earned the good grade she made.

Kaila is really cool

Madison is even cooler

Exercise 2.1

Questions for Teachers About Mindset and Differentiation

Respond to the following questions. After you finish, review your responses and reflect on how your mindset affects your classroom decisions. Building administrators can use this activity at a faculty meeting to discuss how teacher mindset can affect the students' progress in the school. Both teachers and administrators should consider ways in which the school environment and procedures generally reflect a fixed or growth mindset in teachers and students, and the implications of their conclusions. Over time, it is important to carefully examine ways in which both the school and its classrooms can increasingly reflect a growth mindset.

1. How comfortable are you with classes that group students by perceived ability?

2. What evidence have you had in your teaching that students who have previously been seen as "not smart" can be quite successful academically as a result of their effort and a teacher's partnership?

3. When a student does poorly in class, do you ever attribute that to the student's home or background?

4. In what ways do you demonstrate to your students that they are in charge of their academic success—that their effort is the key to their success?

5. How often do you make comments that emphasize being smart versus working hard?

6. In what ways do you show students that discoveries and insights almost inevitably stem from failures rather than from successes?

Differentiation and the Brain • © 2011 Solution Tree Press • solution-tree.com
Visit **go.solution-tree.com/instruction** to download this page.

7. To what degree do you see a student's Ds and Fs as inevitable?

8. To what degree do you see a student's straight As as an indicator that the student may not be experiencing appropriate challenge—may not be growing?

9. How do you share your own failures and persistence with students to ensure that they see you as an adult who believes that continued effort will win the day?

10. In what ways do you monitor your students' mindsets and help them with goal setting and progress monitoring to ensure that each of them will develop a growth mindset about learning and success?

Possible Changes to Consider

Differentiation and the Brain • © 2011 Solution Tree Press • solution-tree.com

Visit **go.solution-tree.com/instruction** to download this page.

Exercise 2.2

Questions for Teachers About Student Affective Needs, Learning Environment, and Differentiation

Respond to the following questions. After you finish, review your responses and reflect on whether you should consider making any changes to your instructional approach in order to meet the affective needs of your students. Building administrators can use this activity at a faculty meeting to discuss the school's progress in working toward the goal of meeting students' affective needs.

Physiological Needs

1. Are you alert to needs such as hunger and sleep deprivation?

2. Do you address those needs for the short term, when appropriate?

3. Do you work with others to address those needs for the longer term?

Need for Safety and Security

4. Are you attuned to student behaviors that might indicate a lack of safety and security at home? Are you prepared to seek competent assistance in working with students who exhibit such behaviors?

5. Do you persistently model respect for each student in all of your actions and comments?

6. Is it clear that you value diversity in the classroom?

7. Is the classroom a tease-free, bully-free, disrespect-free zone?

8. Are there clear classroom rules that emphasize what students *should* do rather than what they *shouldn't* do?

9. Is humor always positive—that is, no sarcasm?

10. Are students called on equitably?

Need for Belonging, Respect, and Affection

11. Do you greet or otherwise connect with each student every day?

12. Do students contribute to developing classroom rules and routines?

13. Do you take time to briefly share your experiences?

14. Do you give students time to share their experiences?

15. Do students listen to you and to one another, and do you listen to students?

Differentiation and the Brain • © 2011 Solution Tree Press • solution-tree.com

Visit **go.solution-tree.com/instruction** to download this page.

16. Do students have regular opportunities to collaborate in the classroom?

17. Do you help students learn how to collaborate effectively?

18. Are problems dealt with respectfully and seen as opportunities to learn and grow?

19. Is everyone expected to contribute to the classroom and supported in doing so effectively?

20. Do you take time to seek the students' input on how class is working for them individually and as a group?

21. Do you seek varied perspectives on topics, issues, and problems?

Need for Achievement and Esteem

22. Do you acknowledge and celebrate legitimate student successes?

23. Do you emphasize competition against oneself rather than competition against one another?

Possible Changes to Consider

Differentiation and the Brain • © 2011 Solution Tree Press • solution-tree.com
Visit **go.solution-tree.com/instruction** to download this page.

Reflections on Cognitive Traits of Learners and the Environments That Support Those Traits

Teachers and administrators should consider whether the environments of their classrooms and schools support the learning traits that we now know about (National Research Council, 1999). Building administrators can use this activity at a faculty meeting to discuss the school's progress in working toward offering students positive learning environments.

Because we know that . . .	Class and school environments should . . .
Children and young people are active learners	Support meaning-making versus absorption of content
Learners construct their own meaning and learn what they come to understand	Promote active involvement in learning
Students naturally set goals, plan, and revise	Call on and continually develop goal-setting, planning, and revision skills
Each student works within a zone or band-width of readiness and competence	Provide for variance in student readiness
Students grow in readiness as they are supported by others in developing the new competencies they need to move ahead	Provide supportive peer and teacher partnerships focused on a particular student's next steps in growth
Students have different learning predispositions, so they learn in different ways	Be flexible enough to emphasize students' various strengths and work with their various weaknesses
Students of the same age learn on different timetables	Be flexible enough to address students' varied needs for practice
Students develop multiple strategies for solving problems gradually, and with practice and guidance	Promote experimenting with solutions and provide plenty of practice time for developing, understanding, selecting, and refining solutions
Students learn best in communities	Provide many and varied opportunities for students to work collaboratively and to develop the skills and attitudes necessary to do so
Students learn best with many tools, artifacts, and materials to support their learning	Be rich in tools, materials, artifacts, and other resources

Exercise 2.4

Questions for Teachers About Student Cognitive Needs, Learning Environment, and Differentiation

Respond to the following questions. After you finish, review your responses and reflect on whether you should consider making any changes to your instructional approach in order to meet the cognitive needs of your students. Building administrators can use this activity at a faculty meeting to discuss the school's progress in working toward the goal of meeting students' cognitive needs.

1. What evidence suggests that the learning environment in your classroom supports student-centered thinking and planning?

2. What elements in the environment in your classroom open the way to dealing with student variance in readiness?

3. In what ways does the environment in your classroom tap into and extend student interests?

4. How does the environment in your classroom offer a variety of ways to explore and express ideas?

5. In what ways does the environment in your classroom acknowledge and encourage attention to student differences in language, culture, gender, and economic status?

6. What structures, routines, and procedures do you use to help students understand, accept, value, and support their commonalities and differences as learners?

Differentiation and the Brain • © 2011 Solution Tree Press • solution-tree.com

Visit **go.solution-tree.com/instruction** to download this page.

7. What routines and procedures do you use to help students develop awareness of themselves as learners and consistently increase their skills and habits of mind as effective learners and problem solvers?

8. What structures and procedures do you use to enable students to work collegially and to contribute effectively to a community of learners?

9. To what degree do materials and other resources in your classroom contribute to student engagement, understanding, and success?

10. What indicators suggest the flexible use of space, time, groupings, resources, strategies, and materials in your classroom to address variability in student needs?

Possible Changes to Consider

Differentiation and the Brain • © 2011 Solution Tree Press • solution-tree.com
Visit **go.solution-tree.com/instruction** to download this page.

CHAPTER 3

Curriculum and Differentiation

Overall, learner-centered environments include teachers who are aware that learners construct their own meanings, beginning with the beliefs, understandings, and cultural practices they bring to the classroom. If teaching is conceived as constructing a bridge between the subject matter and the student, learner-centered teachers keep a constant eye on both ends of the bridge.

—National Research Council, *How People Learn: Brain, Mind, Experience, and School*

While differentiation is an instructional approach, it is counterproductive and artificial to separate curriculum and instruction. They are tightly intertwined in the classroom. The nature of *what* we teach (curriculum) sharply affects the impact of *how* we teach (differentiation). Creating multiple pathways for students to work with insipid and ill-defined curriculum is hardly worth the effort. In addition, the quality of the curriculum communicates clearly to students our level of regard for them and for their potential. Strong curriculum is also a teacher's ally in enlisting student motivation to learn. If curriculum is flat and uninspired, it's difficult for any other classroom element to be dynamic and robust.

The Importance of a Quality Curriculum

The word *curriculum* stems from the Latin word for the course that a person would run on foot or travel by chariot. Over time, it evolved to mean a course of experiences a young person would traverse in order to become an adult. We still refer to a *course* of study. Now, however, we think of curriculum as a planned series of experiences designed to ensure that students achieve designated objectives deemed to be important in a particular segment of content. While a solid curriculum includes methods and strategies for teaching and learning, those plans are enacted only in the instructional phase of teaching. Thus curriculum centers on planning, and instruction focuses on the implementation of those plans.

A Case in Point

The students in Mr. Carnahan's social studies class spent a lot of time studying different cultures. Mr. Carnahan always began a unit on a new culture by providing students with a vocabulary list they would need to master, giving them a blank map they would need to fill in with key places in the region where the culture was located, and having them read the textbook chapter on that culture. They would answer questions at the end of the chapter; learn about the food, clothing, and housing of the culture; and sometimes even get to eat a little of the traditional food of the culture.

An important game the students played in social studies was called "Fact Factory." The idea was for the students to see how many questions they could answer from a list of questions about a particular culture, as well as how fast they could answer the questions correctly. The questions were ones Mr. Carnahan told them might be on the end-of-year standardized test. The students mostly did the work he asked them to do. However, they found it very difficult to remember so many facts and words about so many cultures.

It is both easy and common to assume that a textbook is a curriculum. It is not. It is a teaching and learning tool that contains information that can be useful in developing curriculum. Likewise, it is easy and common to assume that a list of content standards or objectives is a curriculum. It is not. Rather, it is an organizer around which a curriculum might be built.

Designing a quality curriculum is complex and requires a teacher, or some other curriculum developer, who understands the discipline that the curriculum will represent as well as the students who will study the curriculum. The model of differentiation explored in this book places a high premium on the quality of the curriculum, based on the belief that what students learn will shape who they become, how they view learning itself, and how they interact with the world around them. This model of differentiation also works from the premise that virtually all students should have access to the highest-quality curriculum a school has to offer and that effective differentiation makes such access viable.

> What students learn will shape who they become, how they view learning itself, and how they interact with the world around them.

According to this model of differentiation and to many experts in curriculum design (for example, Erickson, 2007; Tomlinson et al., 2008; Tomlinson & McTighe, 2006; Wiggins & McTighe, 2005), a quality curriculum is one that helps students relate to and make meaning of content so they can retain, apply, transfer, and critique the most important knowledge, ideas, and skills in the disciplines they study. As shown in figure 3.1, a quality curriculum has five important characteristics. It is:

1. Organized around essential content goals

2. Aligned with content goals, assessments, and learning experiences

3. Focused on student understanding

4. Engaging for students

5. Authentic

A discussion of each of these characteristics follows.

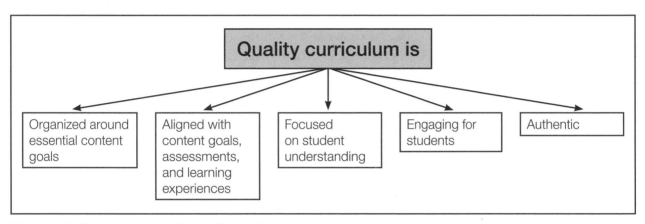

Figure 3.1: Characteristics of a quality curriculum.

Quality Curriculum Is Organized Around Essential Content Goals

Despite the experience of many learners, curriculum is not just a sequence of things students do in a classroom. Despite the early experiences of many teachers, curriculum is not what we think up on Monday night for students to do on Tuesday, on Tuesday night for students to do on Wednesday, and so on. Quality curriculum begins with a set of goals and objectives that represent the essence of the discipline students will study. Further, quality curriculum makes explicit the knowledge, understanding, and skills that students should acquire during a segment of study in order to achieve the specified learning goals. Everything that follows in the curriculum should be in service of ensuring that students learn what they need to achieve the goals.

Most teachers struggle with the reality that there is far too much content to cover in each unit they teach, and consequently in the year as a whole. The state of Hawaii commissioned a study to determine what proportion of a fifth-grade teacher's time would be required to effectively teach the state's required academic standards. Care to guess? The answer was that it would require 3,000 percent of the teacher's time (Wagner, 2008). And that was just for fifth grade! No wonder teachers are racing through the curriculum at every grade level.

Most teachers struggle with the reality that there is far too much content to cover.

Curriculum Races Are Not Brain-Friendly

Curriculum races ensure that course material is covered but not learned. There are two reasons for this result: (1) working memory has a limited capacity, and (2) finding meaning in new learning requires time for reflection. Let's start with working memory—that's the temporary memory where information is consciously processed. Although we had believed since the 1950s that the capacity for working memory was about seven items (plus or minus two) (Miller, 1956), more recent studies have suggested that the capacity may be closer to four items at any one time for adolescents and adults, and probably fewer for preadolescents (Cowan, 2001; Oberauer & Kliegl, 2006). Of course, this number can vary, depending on the learner's motivation and level of distraction. If teachers are racing to cover material, they are likely to present more than four items at once in a lesson. At this point, working memory is at capacity, and any additional information either will be rejected or will replace an item that is already there. As more items enter the lesson, the learner gets frustrated, and the chances that the items will be tagged for long-term storage decrease significantly.

As for finding meaning, we noted earlier that the brain's neural networks are constantly seeking and creating patterns. They do so by analyzing new input to determine if it has some meaningful connection with information already stored in the network. If new learning and understandings are to find a secure place to take hold in the brain's memory network, then they need to make sense, build on past experiences, establish connections, and take meaning from those connections that ultimately emerge. Much meaning comes from pattern making. But making patterns and extending cerebral networks is a reflective and time-consuming process. Racing through the curriculum does not provide that time. Instead of reflecting and building meaning, the brain's efforts are devoted to tagging those isolated bits of information that it perceives as likely to show up on the test.

Note that the two very important words in the preceding paragraph are *sense* and *meaning*. While the brain is attempting to connect new learning to past experiences and form patterns, it must ultimately decide whether this new information will be eventually encoded into long-term memory. This decision seems to be based mainly on two criteria: "Does this make *sense*?" and "Does this have *meaning*?" (Sousa, 2006). The question "Does this make sense?" refers to whether the learner can understand the item on the basis of experience. Does it "fit" into what the learner knows about how the world works? When a student says, "I don't understand," it means the student is having a problem making sense of the learning. The question "Does this have meaning?" refers to whether the item is *relevant* to the learner. For what purpose should the learner remember it? Meaning, of course, is a very personal thing and is greatly influenced by one's own experiences. The same item can have great meaning for one student and none for another. Questions such as

"Why do I have to know this?" or "When will I ever use this?" indicate that the student has not, for whatever reason, accepted the learning as relevant.

For more than a decade, brain scans have confirmed that when new learning is readily comprehensible (makes sense) and can be connected to past experiences (has meaning), there is substantially more cerebral activity, followed by dramatically improved retention (Maguire, Frith, & Morris, 1999; Peelle, Troiani, & Grossman, 2009). Figure 3.2 illustrates that the probability of storing information is directly related to the presence of sense and meaning. Whenever the learner's working memory decides that an item does not make sense or have meaning, the probability of its being stored is extremely low. If either sense or meaning is present, the probability of storage increases significantly. If both sense *and* meaning are present, the likelihood of long-term storage is very high.

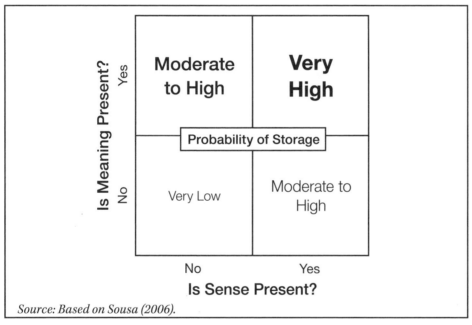

Source: Based on Sousa (2006).

Figure 3.2: The probability of storing information.

Relationship of Sense to Meaning

Sense and meaning are independent of each other. Thus, it is possible to remember an item that makes sense but has no meaning. If you have ever played Trivial Pursuit or a similar game, you may have been surprised at some of the answers you knew. Perhaps another player asked how you knew that answer, and you replied, "I don't know. It was just there!" This happens to all of us. During our lifetime, we pick up bits of information that made sense at the time and, although they were trivial and had no meaning, they made their way into our long-term memory.

It is also possible to remember an item that makes no sense but has meaning. Mathematics is notorious for having rules that students learn because they need them to pass the test (so the learning has meaning). A good example is this rule: when dividing fractions, invert the second term and multiply. No one, except perhaps professional mathematicians, can explain why we "invert the second term and multiply." Thus, for the student, the rule has meaning (I need to know this to pass the test) but does not make sense (Why invert and multiply when I'm supposed to be dividing?). One result of teaching students only the rules but not the sense behind them is that students have no idea how to apply this information to related mathematical operations. Another result is that schools in the United States spend more money on remedial mathematics than on all other forms of mathematics combined (Asher, 2007).

Meaning Is More Significant

Of the two criteria, meaning has the greater impact on the probability that information will be stored. Think of all the television programs you have watched that are *not* stored, even though you devoted one or two hours to them. A particular show's content or story line made sense to you, but if meaning was absent, you just did not save it. It was *entertainment*, and little or no learning resulted from it. You might have remembered a summary of the show, or whether it was enjoyable or boring, but not the details. On the other hand, if the story reminded you of a personal experience, then meaning was present, and you were likely to remember more details of the program.

Teachers spend about 90 percent of their planning time devising lessons so that students will make sense of the learning objective. But to convince a learner's brain to persist with that objective, teachers need to be more mindful of helping students establish meaning. We should also remember that what was meaningful for us as children may not necessarily be meaningful for children today. If we expect students to find meaning, we need to be certain that today's curriculum contains connections to *their* past experiences, not just ours. Furthermore, the enormous size and the strict separation of secondary curriculum areas do little to help students find the time to make relevant connections between and among subjects. Helping students make connections between subject areas by integrating the curriculum increases meaning and retention, especially when students recognize a future use for the new learning (Sousa, 2006).

Specificity Is Important

A curriculum that specifies essential knowledge, understanding, and skills points teachers and their students to where their time and efforts should be invested. It sends the signal that ensuring that students do the really important things well is far more beneficial than reinforcing the prevailing sense that teaching is more about coverage than about learning. This sort of organized framework, which sharpens the teacher's focus on what is essential in the teaching/learning process, should be shared with students as well. Such a framework gives students a sense of direction in learning, making it far more likely that everyone will end up at a known destination than at an unknown one.

Nonetheless, many students (and their teachers) have the experience of watching curriculum just sort of happen day by day until a unit of study (or even a year) is finished. At the end of such a time, it would probably be humbling for the teacher to ask the students to explain what they have learned and why it matters. Chances are, there would be little consensus among class members about what matters most. If students do not know where the teacher is going, then any place will do. Quality curriculum gives teachers and students alike a compass that points faithfully to their shared destination. It prepares the way for a successful journey.

> If students do not know where the teacher is going, then any place will do.

Quality Curriculum Is Aligned

Derek and some of his friends were puzzled when they did poorly on a high school exam for which they had studied hard. The class was an honors-level class, and it was the first time the five students had ever taken an advanced class. Because they wanted to succeed, they worked with tutors for several days over the school's winter break to prepare for the exam. The tutors, who were graduate students at a local university, were confident that the young men understood the content and were ready for the exam. They, too, were bewildered and disappointed when not a single one of the students fared well on the exam. Discovering the reason for the poor results took some careful work on the part of a school administrator who knew of and supported the students' effort to perform well in an advanced-level class. In the end, the cause of the problem was a common one. The teacher's lectures suggested that one facet of content was most important. The text suggested another aspect was most important. The exam measured something quite different from either; it turned out to be more of an exercise in trivia than a measure of student knowledge and understanding. The problem was one of curriculum misalignment.

What Alignment Means

Curriculum includes several elements. At the very least, most experts would agree that curriculum involves content goals, assessments, and learning experiences. The latter element might be expanded or unpacked to include other elements, such as introductory lessons, closure lessons, materials, teaching activities, learning activities, and so on. Once the essential knowledge, understanding, and skills have been specified for a unit of study, it is critical that they work like a magnet for everything else in the unit. That is, all of the elements in the curriculum are tightly aligned with the goals, knowledge, understanding, and skills (and with one another).

This may seem evident, but misalignment of curricular elements is one of the most common contributors to poor student outcomes. Although few teachers go to class unprepared for the day ahead, their lesson plans are often only loosely coupled with content goals. Sometimes the goals are not explicitly stated. Sometimes teachers plan activities because students like them or because they have always been a part of the unit, rather than because they are directly aimed at helping students succeed with designated goals. Sometimes students and teachers "chase rabbits" in a class, pursuing a question or an anecdote at length and departing markedly from the lesson's intent.

> Misalignment of curricular elements is one of the most common contributors to poor student outcomes.

Curriculum is not, and should not be, a "heads-forward-never-look-to-the-left-or-right" proposition. Nonetheless, it is a matter of great consequence that learning outcomes be wisely chosen, clearly articulated, and then squarely addressed throughout every facet of a unit of study. Within a lesson, introductions, materials, teaching activities, learning activities, lesson closure, and so on should keep the goals as well as the knowledge, understanding, and skills that build on them consistently at center stage. As students are assessed to determine their growth and, ultimately, their level of competence with the goals, there should again be perfect alignment with the knowledge, understanding, and skills specified as the reason for the lesson or unit.

Rubrics and other indicators of quality for student work should also be tightly aligned with the designated goals. An effective rubric will lead students to focus on what they need to demonstrate they know, understand, and can do, not on how many pages a paper is, the quality of its cover design, or whether it is typed versus handwritten.

When all aspects of curriculum are aligned with what matters most for students to know, understand, and be able to do, outcomes are predictably better. It is a simple yet elusive principle.

Quality Curriculum Focuses on Student Understanding

Sadly, for many students, learning is an exercise in memorizing data and practicing skills out of context. Students memorize names of states, provinces, or countries and their capitals; parts of the human body; parts of speech; names of literary works and their authors; names of battles and generals; vocabulary lists; and even the periodic table. They also practice using proper punctuation, doing math computations correctly, finding latitude and longitude, and writing a paragraph. Regrettably, however, students lose a great deal of what they memorize, often in a short period of time. Similarly, skills that are practiced without leading to student reasoning have a short shelf life. In both instances, the student's brain is unable to detect in the new learning the patterns or meaning necessary for long-term retention.

As adults, the same students would probably find it difficult to pass the high school and college exams on which they once made good grades. Although their grades suggested they had learned the content, it left them quickly. The chances are also high that many of these seemingly successful students left school without understanding the lessons of history, grasping the power of systems in science, seeing math as a language for reasoning, or realizing that writing is a way to explore the world. Noted one student in an English class when an observer asked what she was writing about, "It doesn't matter. We don't write about anything. We just write."

Quality curriculum supports student understanding by helping students construct *frameworks of meaning* around what some call "concepts and principles" and others call "big ideas." In either case, these are the meaning-making structures that guide the thinking and work of experts in a discipline. The student who comes to understand the living cell as a system with interdependent parts has more durable and useful knowledge than does the student who only memorizes the parts of a cell and places them on a drawing. The student who understands history as a cycle with its roots in the past and ripples into the future no longer sees disconnected chapters in a history book.

Students who use frameworks of understanding can answer questions such as:

- How does this content hang together to make sense? (Do I understand it?)

- How is this content meaningful to me? (Do I relate to it?)

- How do experts organize their thinking about this subject?

- How do other people use the ideas in this subject?

Interestingly, when students organize their thinking around concepts and principles or big ideas, they also retain information and apply skills more readily, because the information has something to adhere to. Understandings are the glue that holds the pieces of the curriculum together.

An understanding-based curriculum also requires students to think deeply and process what they are learning. It does not allow them simply to retain, repeat, or reproduce information, ideas, or skills. Rather, it calls on students to argue with, look from multiple perspectives at, create something novel from, analyze the parts of, solve a problem with, and determine the worth of what they are learning. In this way, what they learn belongs to them rather than being on loan from a teacher or a textbook.

> Understandings are the glue that holds the pieces of the curriculum together.

Learning Tasks Should Extend Understandings

The most powerful tasks ask students to use essential knowledge and essential skills to explore or extend an essential understanding. Knowledge and skills are not sacrificed, as teachers sometimes fear they might be, to achieve understanding. Rather, they are used in service of making meaning. Students who work consistently with such tasks are likely to learn more, retain more, apply their learning more naturally, and transfer what they learn more readily than students who simply attempt to master knowledge and skills out of context. Here is an example.

Students in a primary classroom were studying dinosaurs. For a particular lesson, the teacher wanted her students to *know* the names of some dinosaurs as well as key vocabulary words, such as *habitat* and *adaptation*. She wanted them to *understand* that patterns help us make predictions—specifically, that patterns in animals' bodies can help us predict how they move and eat. What she wanted them to *do* was to look at key features of dinosaurs' bodies, predict how particular dinosaurs would move and eat, and give the reasons behind their thinking.

The teacher divided the class into teams of three or four students and distributed a dinosaur model to each team. The team members had to examine (analyze) the legs, feet, and body shape of their dinosaur to decide (predict) how it would move about. They then examined the neck and mouth of the dinosaur to predict what kind of food it would eat. The class as a whole then shared ideas and gave evidence to vote for or against the idea that patterns help us make predictions.

In this instance, the students used key vocabulary and the skills of analysis and prediction to arrive at, or expand their awareness of, the understanding that patterns help people make good predictions. The knowledge, understanding, and skills worked together to help the students make meaning while they learned key content.

While all students worked with the essential knowledge, understanding, and skills for the lesson, the teacher differentiated in several ways. She gave some students dinosaurs whose body types more clearly predicted their ways of moving and sources of food. She gave others dinosaurs whose body types were a little more ambiguous. She gave some students a set of step-by-step directions for the task, as well as an organizer for recording their predictions. She gave others only a general set of directions and no organizer. Some groups had only three students in them, while some had four. One group only had two. Some groups had vocabulary lists on their tables while others did not. All the teacher's decisions were *purposeful* and were based on her understanding both of student readiness for the task and of the learning conditions that worked best for various students. Her goal in differentiating was to ensure success with the essential knowledge, understanding, and skills, not to change the key learning outcomes.

Understandings Build Neural Networks

Deep learning helps the brain build those important patterns of understanding that were mentioned earlier in this chapter—patterns that are necessary if we expect the new learning to be encoded into long-term memory and recalled when needed. By manipulating the new learning in various ways through different thought processes and sensory modalities, the learner builds more interconnections within and between neural networks. This mass of interconnections provides multiple pathways for retrieving the new learning from long-term memory. It means that the student will be able to recall the new stored learning more easily (that is, with less neural effort) and more quickly in response to an appropriate prompt.

Here is an example of building neural networks and patterns. When we are first introduced to the concept of mammals, we recognize that they are a type of animal. This information gets connected to other memory networks we already have about animals. Spelling out the word M-A-M-M-A-L puts that information in the brain's specialized language regions. After we learn about the characteristics unique to mammals (they have hair or fur and mammary glands), we can apply that knowledge to determine which animals are mammals. Later, we can build other mental associations with mammals we are familiar with—pets or farm animals. We learn about their life cycle, position in various food chains, and how they fit into the different ecological systems around the planet.

Figure 3.3 (page 56) illustrates some of the multiple connections that could represent a neural network on mammals. This network on mammals is most likely connected to other networks, such as one on all animals. A student's experiences both inside and outside the classroom allow the brain to build multiple and redundant interconnections that lead to very simple and very complex understandings about mammals. Rote memorization, on the other hand, establishes only simple connections that lead to stimulus-response reactions ("A cow is a mammal") rather than cause-and-effect analyses ("How would humans be affected if cows no longer existed?").

Different Pathways to Common Goals

There is an additional reason why a focus on understanding is essential in a differentiated classroom. Students will inevitably vary in their level of skills and their knowledge base. Therefore, in a differentiated classroom, teachers often make time to ensure that students are working individually and in small groups to concentrate on the specific skills and knowledge they need to move ahead. At these times, students are working more as soloists and in small ensembles than as an orchestra. However, all students should be working with the essential understandings in a unit of study (Tomlinson & McTighe, 2006). They may need different support systems, tasks at different levels of complexity, and varied materials to do so, but, with the exception of students whose individual educational plans indicate otherwise, they should share a focus on essential understandings. Thus, conversations and sharing about essential understandings bring the class together as an orchestra of ideas around a common score. If the curriculum focuses only

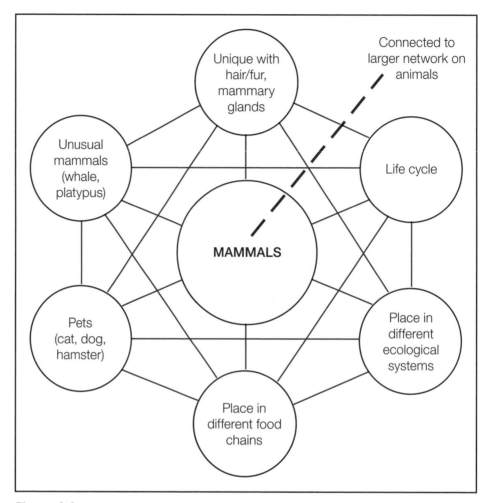

Figure 3.3: A neural network on mammals.

on knowledge and skills, then not only are students in a differentiated class-room (or any classroom) deprived of an opportunity to deeply understand what they are studying, but they are also shortchanged by not being part of a community of learners with shared ideas. Understanding-focused curricu-lum is brain-friendly, differentiation-friendly, and, therefore, learner-friendly.

Quality Curriculum Engages Students

As the bell rang for science class to begin, Mr. Wagner asked students to volunteer to turn a bar with a grip on each end and a bicycle wheel mounted in its center. "You'll need to be strong," he cautioned. Many hands shot into the air. One by one, students tried to move the pole to the right or to the left as the teacher rapidly spun the bicycle wheel. Each new volunteer was sure he or she could accomplish what the previous one hadn't been able to do. No one could move the rod while the bicycle wheel was spinning.

Had the teacher started the class by saying, "Today, we're going to study inertia and momentum. Please take out your notebooks," few of his middle school students would have reacted with enthusiasm. Instead, Mr. Wagner asked himself some important questions as he planned his curriculum. "How do I help the students care about what they need to learn? How do I help them connect it to their lives and experiences?" By helping students both experience and relate to the concepts he wanted them to understand, he increased student interest in what lay ahead and their motivation to understand it.

Sara Kajder (2006) helped discouraged and often angry adolescent students see themselves as readers and writers by having them use technologies that they found relevant (such as blogs, vlogs, and digital portfolios) to explore and express important ideas. Steven Levy (1996) helped his fourth-grade students find relevance in the long-ago lives of the Pilgrims by inviting them to experience some of their lifeways. The students built classroom furniture using only tools that had been available to the Pilgrims. They also made bread and spun yarn for fabric just as the Pilgrims would have. They used the Pilgrims' decision-making processes to address classroom dilemmas. Their direct involvement with a time and place unfamiliar to them greatly enhanced their desire to learn, as well as their success as learners.

Anyone who has taught or raised young children has noticed their innate and persistent desire for discovery. They spend their waking hours chasing, tasting, sniffing, handling, and observing nearly everything in their environment. Their eyes gleam and their chatter increases when they make a new discovery. So it should come as no surprise that neuroscientists believe that the young brain develops neural circuitry specifically for intrinsic motivation—that is, the desire to get information from the environment for the sheer enjoyment of it (Kaplan & Oudeyer, 2007). The implication from this research is that every lesson plan should be a motivational plan (Ginsberg & Wlodkowski, 2000). Quality curriculum motivates students to engage with its essential knowledge, understanding, and skills. It is designed to provide high-relevance learning experiences for the students who will study it and to be pertinent, purposeful, interesting, and useful to them. Relevance increases student motivation to learn and thus opens the way for increased student achievement.

> It seems that the young brain develops neural circuitry specifically for intrinsic motivation.

Quality Curriculum Is Authentic

Based solely on their school experiences, students might conclude that historians are people who go to work each day, read a book, and answer questions at the end of each chapter. They would be equally likely to conclude that scientists are people who set up and conduct experiments someone else designed to figure out answers someone else already knows. Students study about subjects but seldom really engage in a discipline the way an expert would. Thus, they tend not to get a real sense of either the discipline or what it would be like to work with the discipline as a career. Authentic curriculum asks students at least some of the time to be real writers instead of just learning about writing or following a tightly prescribed writing process. It calls on them to propose solutions to environmental or economic problems that have no ready answers instead of just studying ecology and economics in textbooks.

There is a close connection between curriculum that promotes understanding, curriculum that engages students, and curriculum that is authentic. Authentic curriculum clearly promotes student thinking and understanding. It also tends to engage students because of its obvious relevance to the real world. While authentic curriculum is likely to support understanding and engagement, not all curriculum that supports understanding and engagement is authentic. Authentic curriculum casts students in the roles of problem solvers and creators of knowledge rather than mere consumers of knowledge, and it has at least four key characteristics that tie into what holds the brain's focus and interest:

1. It calls on students to use knowledge as an expert would (establishes meaning for the present).

2. It asks students to work on the kinds of complex and ambiguous problems an expert would address (establishes meaning for the future).

3. It asks students to use the skills an expert uses (promotes interest).

4. It helps students focus on the habits of mind and work necessary for quality in a field (makes connections to past knowledge and facilitates transfer of learning).

Our two "In the Classroom" scenarios illustrate these features of an authentic curriculum. In both examples, the students change their sense of themselves as learners, deepen their understanding of content, and develop an awareness of learning as a living process that directly affects people's lives. Authentic curriculum ensures that students experience knowledge at work in the world.

In the Classroom

Hosting International Students (Primary Grades)

Ms. Glassner asked her primary-grade students to develop plans for hosting some children from another country who would be at their school for a week. The plans had to make effective use of a five-hour day to ensure that the guests would learn about the students' town and their school. A culminating task at the end of a unit on time, this project called on students to tell time, estimate time, and use time at a wide range of intervals. The problem was fuzzy and open-ended, and it required students to be flexible in their thinking. In the end, the students reviewed all the proposed itineraries and invited their guests to choose from several that seemed likely to help them experience the area they were visiting. The students came to understand the purpose and uses of time at a deeper level than had they simply completed worksheets and class exercises on time.

In the Classroom
Exploring Traffic Patterns (Middle School)

Ms. Harrington showed her students the traffic flow patterns projected for a new school site near the middle school they attended. As they examined how cars and buses would enter the school grounds, they noticed that the projected patterns seemed to pose some potentially dangerous situations. Over an extended period, while continuing to work with the prescribed curriculum in class, the students studied traffic patterns in the new site and ultimately proposed alternatives to the local governing agencies. In the process, the students had to understand how surveyors worked, read blueprints, consider the economic implications of the options they devised, and use many more mathematical operations than they would ever bring together in a classroom. They also learned a great deal about government, public speaking, and diplomacy. One student noted, "I never knew math happened outside of class. This year, it had a life of its own!"

This project clearly engaged students and caused them to think about and understand mathematics at a new level. It also required them to make connections across content areas that had previously been segmented in school, understand and apply expert thinking within and across disciplines, challenge current thinking, engage in collaboration, find new resources and information sources, tolerate ambiguity, propose new solutions, evaluate their work according to expert criteria, and defend their thinking, to name a few dimensions of their experience.

Differentiating Quality Curriculum

Effectively differentiated curriculum will first be effective curriculum. In other words, it will clearly define what students must know, understand, and be able to do as the result of any segment of study—a day, a week, a unit, a year. All elements of the curriculum will be designed to focus the teacher and students on the essential outcomes. A key characteristic of the curriculum will be its emphasis on students as thinkers who genuinely understand what they are learning. Quality curriculum will also be highly relevant to students so as to enlist their motivation to learn. Finally, quality curriculum will engage students in the discipline in authentic ways that approximate the ways in which experts in the discipline work. Exercise 3.1 (page 61) offers some questions that teachers might use to think about the quality of a curriculum unit.

Effectively differentiated curriculum then adds one more characteristic to this set: it is developed with student variances in mind. That is, it is planned to account for different levels of reading and writing proficiency, different readiness levels, different interests, and different preferences for learning. Ideally, one begins not by developing quality curriculum and then differentiating it, but rather by anticipating student differences and incorporating ways to respond to those differences as the curriculum is developed.

Effectively differentiated curriculum is developed with student variances in mind.

A Better Scenario

Mr. Carnahan began the year by asking students to complete a "culture circles" exercise. Each student used a graphic organizer with overlapping circles to show the cultures they were members of and arrows to show how the cultures in their lives influenced one another. Lei Wan, for example, said she was a member of the Chinese culture, a family culture, and the school culture. She explained that a Chinese belief in hard work shaped her family's expectation that she would study hard. In turn, that expectation influenced her image in school as a serious student. "I might not be so serious about school if my family were not so Chinese," she said.

Throughout the year, Mr. Carnahan challenged his students to find both confirming and contradictory evidence for the statement "A culture shapes the people in it, and the people in it shape the culture." He helped them see interrelationships between cultural elements such as geography, economy, communication, technology, social groups, beliefs and customs, roles, stories, and heroes. He asked them to try to connect their own cultural experiences to the cultures they learned about, to look for patterns of similarity and difference among cultures, and to think about why the patterns exist. He always encouraged them to use critical vocabulary in their conversations and work.

Ashram said, "I remember what I learn in here because I see how all the parts fit together." Britt said, "I tell my parents what we're learning in class when we talk about the news at home. They're surprised how many things I connect with social studies."

Exercise 3.1

Questions for Teachers About the Quality of a Curriculum Unit

Respond to the following questions. After you finish, review your responses and reflect on whether you should consider making any changes to the curriculum unit in order to meet the needs of the full range of your students. Building administrators can use this activity at a faculty meeting to discuss the school's progress in working toward offering all students a quality curriculum, as well as the importance of having a quality curriculum in place as a platform for addressing the diverse needs of students in the school.

1. In unit and lesson planning, do I consistently state what students should know, understand, and be able to do as a result of the unit as a whole and as a result of each lesson in the unit?

2. Is the unit constructed so that students will consistently be aware of what they should know, understand, and be able to do as a result of each segment of work and as a result of the unit as a whole?

3. Is the unit constructed to ensure high relevance to students' lives and experiences so that they can build new knowledge on the prior knowledge or experience they bring to the classroom?

4. Does a substantial portion of what I present to students in the unit help them make meaning of what they are trying to learn?

5. Does a substantial portion of the work I ask students to do in the unit help them make meaning of what they are trying to learn?

page 1 of 2

Differentiation and the Brain • © 2011 Solution Tree Press • solution-tree.com

Visit **go.solution-tree.com/instruction** to download this page.

6. Does a substantial portion of the unit help students understand how the discipline works?

7. Does the unit ensure that students regularly use essential knowledge and essential skills to explore, apply, or expand on essential understandings?

8. Are class presentations, student tasks, and student assessments tightly aligned with the unit's goals (essential knowledge, understanding, and skills)?

9. Does the work that I ask my students to do help them understand how experts use important content to address problems and how the content makes a difference in the world?

10. Does the work that I ask my students to do generally support them in becoming thinkers and problem solvers, often drawing on the methods and practices of experts?

Possible Changes to Consider

Differentiation and the Brain • © 2011 Solution Tree Press • solution-tree.com

Visit **go.solution-tree.com/instruction** to download this page.

CHAPTER 4

Classroom Assessment and Differentiation

Most of the kids never talk about it, but a lot of the time bad grades make them feel dumb, and almost all the time it's not true. And good grades can make other kids think that they're better, and that's not true either. And then all the kids start competing and comparing. The smart kids feel smarter and better and get all stuck-up, and the regular kids feel stupid and like there's no way to ever catch up. And the people who are supposed to help kids . . . they don't.

—Andrew Clements, *The Report Card*

Teachers often use assessment predominantly to determine who "got" what was taught and who did not "get" it, so that they can record a lengthy string of grades to back up what appears on the report card. As a result, assessment becomes almost synonymous with grading, and teachers lament, "If I don't grade the work, the students won't do it." Both teachers and students begin to see assessment as a system to mete out rewards and punishment. Some students become acclimated to continual rewards and balk when the supply of them is threatened. Other students accept assessment data as evidence that they will never succeed in school, and their motivation to continue to put forth the effort to learn erodes and ultimately disappears.

Luggage From the Past: Negative Images of Classroom Assessment

Our brain is programmed in such a way that what we learn and retain during our years as children and adolescents gets well consolidated into our long-term memory sites (Squire & Kandel, 1999). During this time, the young brain is building networks and developing a grand view of how the world works and how we believe we can survive in it. This cognitive belief system becomes part of our persona and influences the way we respond to the people and situations in our environment. Beliefs and attitudes in this system are not easily changed, because they were made at a time when we were very impressionable, and they were often rehearsed and reinforced by our caregivers and others. This staying power is evidenced by the biases and prejudices that young people learn and carry with them their entire lives.

A Case in Point

Darius is working hard to do well in his classes. Doing his homework is a challenge because he has to take care of his younger brothers in the evening, but he is finding the time, even though it often means staying up late. Two of his classes are especially discouraging, however. In one class, he just can't figure out what's going to be on the test. Some kids in the class seem to have the knack of reading the teacher's mind, but not Darius—at least not yet. He feels like he knows what the teacher talks about in class and what's in the textbook, but the tests always seem to be about something else. In the other class, the content is hard for him. He nearly always makes at least a B on the final exam. His teacher tells him it's too bad his pop quiz and test grades early in the marking period are low, because that pulls down his good exam grade. He's really discouraged and thinks maybe he just can't be a good student—or maybe those teachers don't like him.

All new teachers enter the profession after engaging in what Dan Lortie, a noted educator and sociologist, describes as a long "apprenticeship of observation" that shapes their thinking about classrooms—almost indelibly (Lortie, 2002, p. 61). That apprenticeship is not the college or university education program. It is not the student teaching experience. Rather, it is the roughly 13,000 hours that prospective teachers spend as K–12 students. During those years, they may be studying mathematics, literature, art, or a host of other subjects, but they are also developing profound and generally unarticulated impressions about how school works. The efforts of teacher preparation programs to reform novice teachers' thinking about how classrooms should work often pale in comparison to the young educators' powerful and entrenched images of how classrooms do work. There may be no greater evidence of teachers' K–12 enculturation about teaching than prevailing notions about the nature and purposes of assessment in the classroom.

Many young educators begin their first teaching assignment with a view of classroom assessment that includes elements of weaponry and harsh justice. They bring from their past a logic that suggests that assessment is testing, testing is about grading, and grading is about distinguishing winners and losers. Teachers, Lortie (2002) notes, conclude from their apprenticeship of observation that they fill gradebooks with test scores for two major purposes: (1) to justify report card grades to parents, students, and potentially to principals and (2) as a tool (maybe a weapon) to make sure students do the work they are asked to do.

> Many young educators begin their first teaching assignment with a view of classroom assessment that includes weaponry and harsh justice.

In addition, teachers often import into their own teaching the belief that there is supposed to be a "gotcha" element in assessment. This belief is based on their own experience of assessment as a cat-and-mouse game in which the teacher is secretive about what will be on a test. The "good students" figure out how to second-guess the teacher. Less successful ones just cannot detect the teacher's pattern and so do not know what to study to prepare for tests. But even the best students get "caught" when the teacher purposely includes obscure items that no student is likely to be prepared for. Then the teacher can say, "Gotcha! I'm always the cleverest person in the room."

Grading practices, too, are often imports from an unquestioned past. Our school mission statements insist that we believe that all students can learn, but we grade as though we are somehow better teachers if many of them do not. While grades motivate some bright learners, they often motivate them to pursue grades rather than to learn deeply. For those students, learning becomes a drug that increases their appetite for more drugs. For many other students, grades are repeated reminders that they are not good enough and thus harden the core of a fixed mindset (Earl, 2003; O'Connor, 2007). Grading practices, in fact, often alienate students from the central mission of schooling.

The baggage related to classroom assessment and grading that teachers often bring to their work almost inevitably includes a sense that assessment and judgment are inextricably intertwined. Some teachers like the role of judge. Some find it in conflict with their goal of being a student's mentor and advocate. In either case, a kind of negativity that helps neither students nor teachers—and is definitely not brain-friendly—hovers around the concept of assessment.

Testing and Stress

Testing of all kinds creates stress because many students perceive testing as a judgment of their intelligence. Students are under greater stress when they take summative assessments than when they take formative assessments because they know that summative assessments generally carry far greater weight in determining their grades and performance.

Stress and Recall

We already noted in chapter 2 that stress produces cortisol—the hormone that directs the brain's attention to the source of the stress. So instead of concentrating on providing the cognitive information required by the test questions, some of the brain's neural efforts are now committed to the emotional task of worrying about the individual's test score and its implications. As a result, the student's performance on the test is very likely to be lower than it would have been without the stress.

There is another important reason why common assessment procedures do not reflect what information the students have really remembered. What teacher has not had the experience of giving a test in which most of the class did well and then discovering several weeks later that the students have almost no recall of what was on that test? How can that happen, especially when there has long been substantial research evidence (see, for example, Chan, 2009; Karpicke & Zaromb, 2010) that every time we recall information from long-term memory, we relearn it? This recall and rehearsal during assessment is known as the "testing effect," but it presumes that the information was already stored in long-term memory. We now know that working memory (a temporary memory) can actually hold information for longer than we thought, perhaps for up to several weeks, and discard it when no longer needed. Students in a fast-paced, assessment-driven classroom environment have learned to carry information in working memory just long enough to take the test, after which it promptly fades away. Because they cannot recall what they have not retained, it is no surprise that they have little or no memory of that information later on.

What About Timed Tests?

Timed tests also produce stress for many students. Their brains often get so preoccupied with the time limits that their cortisol levels begin to interfere with the simple recall of how, for example, to organize a persuasive piece of writing (Petersen, 2009) or carry out simple mathematics operations (Tsui & Mazzocco, 2007). The more we learn about the brain, the more we can question the benefit of timed tests in everyday classroom assessments. While no one proposes giving students totally unlimited time for an assessment, the notion that one must produce an answer quickly runs counter to our understanding of how memory systems are activated and respond in different individuals.

Some students' memory systems are so well organized and networked that their response time is fast. Others' memory systems are not so well consolidated and contain weaker links. This does not mean that the student with the weaker links does not know the correct response. Rather, it means that it will probably take longer to retrieve it, even when the student is *not* under stress. If the purpose of assessment is to determine what the student knows, where is the logic in messing up an already delayed retrieval process by pumping cortisol into the system to add further interference? Timed tests may be appropriate for certain competitions and for standardized tests, but educators need to reevaluate their purpose in the daily instructional environment.

> Timed tests may be appropriate for certain competitions and for standardized tests, but educators need to reevaluate their purpose in the daily instructional environment.

A More Productive View of Assessment

Experts who have invested their careers in understanding effective assessment practices (for example, Earl, 2003; Reeves, 2007; Stiggins, 2001; Wiggins, 1993, 1998) paint a very different image of classroom assessment from the one described at the beginning of this chapter. Rather than see assessment predominantly as a tool for judgment, they regard it as an opportunity for reflection. Rather than present it as shrouded in mystery, they promote it as an exercise in clarity. Rather than cast it as wholly in the jurisdiction of the teacher, they emphasize the central role of the student in assessment. The real goal of classroom assessment is to improve student performance, not merely to audit it (Wiggins, 1998).

All of these experts begin with the premise that the teacher's job is to vigorously and persistently support the success of each student as a learner. Virtually every element in the classroom should be a tool to facilitate that goal. High-quality curriculum, they remind us, exists for that purpose, as does a positive classroom environment. Likewise, the rightful role of assessment is to help students succeed. If we use the yardstick of supporting student success as a measure of effective assessment practices, then we quickly see that the mystery, harsh judgment, external motivation, and trickery that many teachers experienced in their own schooling fall short. Assessment should not be used to categorize students, but to push their learning forward (Earl, 2003).

What are the attributes of effective assessment practices? Again, most of the experts in classroom assessment agree that, at a minimum, assessment practices should reflect the following principles:

- Targets of effective classroom assessments are absolutely clear to the teacher. That is, they align absolutely with the essential knowledge, essential understanding, and essential skills delineated by a high-quality curriculum. They are designed to reflect a clear sense of the teacher's expectations for quality performance. Stiggins (2001) advises,

  > If your job is to teach students to become better writers, you should start with a highly refined vision of what good writing looks like and a sense of how to help your students meet that standard. If your mission is to promote math problem-solving, you had better be a confident, competent master of that performance domain yourself. Without a sense of the final destination reflected in your standards, and signposts along the way against which to check students' progress, you will have difficulty being an effective teacher. (p. 19)

- Targets of effective classroom assessments are absolutely clear to the students. Students in classrooms that exhibit effective instructional practices are not surprised by the contents of assessments. Rather, they work toward well-defined targets of knowledge, understanding, and skills and know that they will be the focus of assessments. When students study hard only to discover that the teacher assessed or tested something unexpected, they learn two lessons: effort does not pay off, and teachers are not to be trusted (Guskey, 2007). Neither lesson benefits student success or fosters a positive classroom climate.

- Effective classroom assessments are appropriate for their intended use.

The real goal of classroom assessment is to improve student performance, not merely to audit it.

- They are the right kind of assessment to measure what needs to be measured. For example, a multiple-choice test may be an appropriate way to assess knowledge, but it will seldom be an effective way to measure student understanding.

- Items on the assessment are a fair sample of the content to be assessed. For example, an assessment should not stress the teacher's favorite aspects of a segment of knowledge and fail to measure student proficiency with other equally important aspects of the topic.

- The assessment emphasizes what matters most in the topic of study. This principle suggests that assessments will focus in large measure on student understanding, not simply on recall of information or display of decontextualized skills, because, as we have noted before, students do not really learn what they do not understand.

- The assessment works for the students who will use it. For example, if an assessment reflects cultural bias, it may work against students who, for various reasons, are sensitive to that bias. Likewise, if the assessment requires writing an essay to demonstrate knowledge of a scientific process, a student with a learning disability that affects writing or a student whose first language is other than the language of the classroom will most likely perform poorly on the assessment, even if that student understands the scientific process in question. Effective classroom assessments, then, maximize the opportunity for students to demonstrate what they know, understand, and can do.

- Effective classroom assessments employ clear communication. The teacher makes sure not only that the targets of the assessment are clear throughout the instructional cycle that precedes the assessment but also that the assessment itself models clear communication. Both written and oral directions must be clear to the students so that the parameters and expectations for quality are transparent. Clear feedback after an assessment is also critical to ensure that assessment supports student learning. An "86" or a "D" at the top of a paper does little to help a student improve his or her performance. Vague comments such as "Nice job" are not instructionally beneficial either. By contrast, a comment such as the following helps a student understand where his or her work hit preestablished targets and where it missed: "Your topic sentence is clear, and it engaged me as a reader. Your first three supporting ideas in the paragraph flow logically from the topic sentence. I am less clear, however, on how the final supporting detail in the paragraph supports the idea in the topic sentence. An additional sentence might clarify your thinking for your readers."

- Effective classroom assessment practice leads to improved instruction. Guskey (2007) explains, "Assessments provide teachers with specific evidence in their efforts to improve the quality of their teaching by helping them identify what they taught well and what needs work" (p. 18). Teachers who continually refine their practice do not just grade assessments (or even just give feedback) and move on. They use what they learn from assessments about student mastery of essential knowledge, understanding, and skills to refine or revise their teaching plans in the near term (Guskey, 2007). Effective practice ensures that assessments are not the end of the line but consistently spark new beginnings for teachers and students.

- Students are key beneficiaries of effective classroom assessment practices. In chapter 2, we discussed the importance of tending to students' affective needs. Over time, effective assessment practices actually contribute to students' sense of emotional safety in the classroom (Earl, 2003). They do so in the following ways:

  - Effective assessment practices help students prepare to succeed by making clear to them from the outset of an instructional unit what is valued and what quality looks like.

  - The practice of giving timely feedback on assessments coaches students toward success by keeping them focused on critical outcomes and on the attributes of quality. It helps them understand throughout the learning cycle where they are proficient and how they can get better.

  - Effective assessment practices contribute to a fluid or growth mindset in students by proving to them that consistent effort results in consistent success.

  - Effective assessment increases students' ownership of learning and independence. Students learn in various ways by analyzing their own work according to clear criteria, by comparing their own work to quality samples of student work, and by setting goals that lead to increasingly stronger products.

Rather than being something that comes at the end of teaching and learning episodes, assessment, rightly seen, is integral to the success of virtually everything that happens in the classroom. In the end, effective assessment practices improve both teaching and learning (Guskey, 2007). Exercise 4.1 (page 82) offers some questions that teachers might ask to determine whether an assessment is effective in terms of these guidelines.

Effective assessment practices improve both teaching and learning.

Purposes of Classroom Assessments

In recent years, educators have begun to distinguish between three purposes of classroom assessment: assessment *of* learning, assessment *for* learning, and assessment *as* learning (Earl, 2003; Stiggins, 2001). All three are valid, but their intent differs.

Assessment of Learning

Assessment of learning is summative in nature. That is, it happens after extended periods of teaching and learning with an eye toward determining who has mastered essential content at those key junctures. In essence, it says, "The students were supposed to get to Chicago. Did they get there?" Summative assessment does have an element of judgment in it because it has a major impact on student grades. However, students will more likely perceive the judgment as appropriate and fair—and therefore less stressful—if the teacher has followed the principles of effective assessment noted earlier: clear goals, appropriate sampling of knowledge, clear communication, freedom from bias, and so on. Summative assessments can take varied forms, such as short-answer tests, essay tests, writing assignments, authentic problems to solve, portfolios, and public presentations. Performance assessments are particularly important for determining student understanding. These assessments ask students to apply what they have learned—to "feed forward" and audition their knowledge, understanding, and skills in unfamiliar and meaningful contexts.

Types of Summative Assessments

Summative assessments fall into two major categories: those that assess rote-knowledge skills and those that assess higher-level executive functions. Most schools generally use rote-knowledge tests because of the traditional notion that they measure all the cognitive skills associated with IQ (Jensen, 1998). They also tend to be easier to grade. But imaging studies in neuroscience since the late 1990s strongly suggest that the brain structures that process rote-knowledge skills are different from those involved in higher-level mental functions, such as creativity and complex problem solving. Closed-end questions that have only one answer evoke rote-knowledge recall, a process referred to as *convergent thinking*. This activity can often occur with little participation of the brain's frontal lobe, where the executive functions are located. However, open-ended questions that have multiple solutions generate higher-level processing. Figure 4.1 illustrates the different brain regions that have the greatest activation during rote recall and higher-level processing. Notice how much more of the brain is involved when it is challenged by open-ended questions (Carter, 1998; Fink, Benedek, Grabner, Staudt, & Neubauer, 2007; Moore et al., 2009).

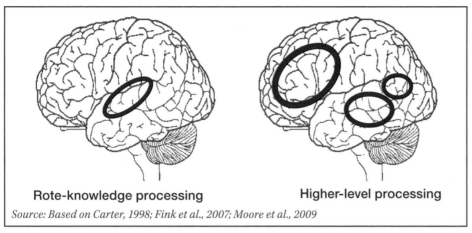

Rote-knowledge processing   Higher-level processing

Source: Based on Carter, 1998; Fink et al., 2007; Moore et al., 2009

Figure 4.1: Brain regions activated during rote-knowledge processing and higher-level processing.

Many states start high-stakes summative testing in the fourth grade. Some researchers contend that too much emphasis on convergent assessment, especially with preadolescent students, is conditioning the brain for rote-knowledge recall at the expense of developing higher-level executive functions (Delis et al., 2007). No one denies that rote skills such as vocabulary, reading, and mathematics are important cognitive abilities for achievement in all aspects of life, including academic advancement and career success. But school-age children and adolescents should continue to receive regular assessments of higher-level executive functions. Our modern society includes a growing number of professions that need individuals with particular strengths in abstract and creative thinking skills to solve our most serious problems. The lack of sufficient assessment tools in schools to assess these higher-level cognitive skills may hinder our ability to steer the best students into these types of careers. By including more assessments of higher-level thinking, we can more accurately identify students with either weaknesses or strengths in executive functions and guide them into the educational programs and career paths that best fit their needs and abilities.

> Emphasis on convergent assessment with preadolescent students is conditioning their brain for rote-knowledge recall at the expense of developing higher-level executive functions.

Another argument for assessing higher-level thinking relates to our earlier discussion of testing and stress. As explained there, in a stressful testing situation, the recall of information to answer a test question is *suppressed* as the brain plans its response to the stress signals. It turns out that this suppression is far easier when just a limited region of the brain is involved, as is the case when a student responds to closed-end questions (see the brain diagram on the left in fig. 4.1). Conversely, the suppression is much more difficult if many brain regions are involved, as is the case when a student responds to an open-ended question (see the brain diagram on the right in fig. 4.1). Recent brain-imaging studies show that when positive emotions are involved, it becomes even more difficult for the cortisol blockade (Buchanan & Tranel, 2008; Sandi & Pinelo-Nava, 2007; Wolf, 2009). This may be because the effects of cortisol are further dampened by the presence of the endorphins associated with positive feelings. In other words, even though summative tests produce stress, the *effects* of the stress may be reduced when the summative assessment contains more questions requiring higher-level thinking and emotional processing—thereby involving more brain areas—than questions evoking just rote recall.

A common adage is "What gets tested gets taught." If this is true, then including higher-level assessments in the regular curriculum plan will encourage teachers to work on higher-level thinking skills with their students. Studies show that these skills can be introduced as a standard part of the curriculum as early as sixth grade and that students who are taught these skills perform better on higher-order thinking assessments than their peers who are not (Burke & Williams, 2008; Glassner & Schwarz, 2007).

Assessment for Learning

Assessment for learning is formative rather than summative. In other words, its purpose is not to determine who succeeded (or who did not), and to what degree, at the end of a lengthy period of teaching and learning. Instead, assessment for learning has a step-by-step focus designed to help both student and teacher arrive at a prescribed destination. It says, "Chicago is the destination. How did today's travel contribute to each student's getting closer to Chicago or turning in a wrong direction?" Formative assessment provides guidance to the student through specific, descriptive feedback from the teacher on how to get back on track or how to move ahead. It provides guidance to the teacher on how to craft instructional plans to help some students get back on track and to help others move ahead from various points of progress. Teachers use preassessments or diagnostic assessments as a unit of study begins to determine the students' various points of entry into new content and to discover those students who may lack prerequisite knowledge that is critical to success in the upcoming unit. Once a unit begins, the teacher systematically uses ongoing assessment to trace the progress of students toward established learning goals.

As is the case with summative assessments, formative assessments should have the characteristics of effective classroom assessments noted earlier. Unlike summative assessments, however, formative assessments should generally not be graded. Formative assessment emphasizes *learning* rather than *grading*. It exists to provide information to teachers and students that will help them build toward success and that will increase the likelihood that each student will know, understand, and be able to do what is required to demonstrate proficiency on a well-crafted summative assessment. Ultimately, formative assessment should enable students not just to perform well on a summative assessment but to use what they have learned in a variety of contexts. Because it has a different function, formative assessment is secondary in importance to summative assessment when determining student grades.

Formative assessment emphasizes *learning* rather than *grading*.

Assessment as *Learning*

Assessment as learning (Earl, 2003) also has a formative emphasis but gives particular importance to the role of the student in coming to own his or her success as a learner. When assessment is used as learning, the goal is to help students do the following:

- Develop the self-awareness and skills necessary to monitor what they are learning

- Ask important questions on their own behalf to support their learning

- Construct meaning

- Use specific teacher feedback to select or adjust strategies that benefit their success

- Relate what they are learning to their own experiences

- Make connections among ideas to extend learning

- Evaluate the worth of ideas

- Determine which information was actually stored in long-term memory and which was not

While assessment for learning and assessment as learning overlap, the latter approach uses assessment not only to contribute to student success on a given topic at a given time but also to build a learner who is increasingly confident, competent, and self-directed. Studies in several countries have shown that formative assessments, especially in high schools, can be potent tools for helping students find ways to raise their achievement levels (Tierney & Charland, 2007). Both assessment for learning and assessment as learning pivot on

- Clear articulation of essential knowledge, understanding, and skills

- Curriculum that is absolutely aligned with the essential knowledge, understanding, and skills

- Instruction and assessment squarely focused on the essential knowledge, understanding, and skills

- Teacher feedback to students that is clear and specific regarding student performance on the essential knowledge and skills

Assessment and Differentiation

As we have pointed out, high-quality or defensible differentiation begins with best practices in a particular area, such as classroom environment or curriculum, and helps teachers adapt those practices to individual learners' needs as well as the needs of the class as a whole. That is true also for assessment practices and differentiation. In other words, defensible differentiation—or differentiation that research suggests is likely to be powerful in supporting student learning—applies the principles of effective classroom assessment noted earlier in the chapter and asks teachers to think about implementing those principles with an eye toward enhancing the likelihood of the success of every learner in the class. Table 4.1 summarizes the kinds and purposes of assessment and suggests the possibilities for differentiation by giving a variety of examples of each kind. It is important to note that many assessment strategies can be used for each kind of assessment. The table is not intended to imply that strategies are limited in their use to one aspect of assessment.

Practitioners of differentiation recognize the following important points about the role of assessment in addressing academic diversity:

- The effective use of preassessment and formative assessment is the prelude to effective differentiation. As Lorna Earl (2003) explains, if a teacher establishes clear learning goals and consistently assesses to see where students are relative to those goals throughout a unit of study, he or she will almost inevitably find that some students already know what is about to be taught, some have both correct and incorrect ideas and information about the topic, some are well behind expectations, and some appear on course. At that point, Earl says, differentiation is not just an option for that teacher; rather, it is the next logical step.

- The effective use of preassessment, formative assessment, and summative assessment is integral to ensuring that students and teachers alike work from a growth mindset—the belief that effort is the key determiner of success. These forms of assessment are powerful tools in helping students focus and maintain focus on critical content, improving step by step with targeted assessment and clear feedback. In that way, assessment mediates student success (Earl, 2003).

- The effective use of preassessment strengthens teacher-student connections because information from the assessments helps teachers learn about students and support their growth. That, in turn, indicates to students that the teacher wants to know them and wants to be a factor in their success. Such a relationship is brain-friendly because feelings of success release the neurochemical dopamine, exciting the brain's reward circuits and increasing the likelihood that students will persist with the learning even when the challenge level increases. We will explore this dopamine-reward circuit more in the next chapter.

- The effective use of preassessment and formative assessment provides instructionally relevant information about student readiness, interest, and learning profile, enabling teachers to develop instructional plans to address all three areas at appropriate points. Furthermore, these assessments reveal to the teacher the prior-knowledge

Table 4.1: Kinds, Purposes, and Examples of Assessments in a Differentiated Classroom

Kind of Assessment	Purpose	Examples
Diagnostic/preassessment (assessment for learning)	To determine a student's point of entry into a unit of study relative to the unit's stated outcomes. Also important in understanding students' interests and learning profiles. Guides the teacher in making early instructional adjustments to address student needs. Never graded.	Guided observations Frayer diagrams Journal entries Short-answer responses Skills surveys Reading samples Writing samples Interest inventories Learning preference checklists
Formative (assessment for learning, assessment as learning)	To provide the teacher with information about student progress at many times in a unit of study so that he or she can adapt instructional plans to close the gap between a student's current knowledge, understanding, and skills and the outcomes designated as necessary for student success. Also provides students with information about their learning relative to goals to enable effective student action on their own behalf. Rarely graded.	Exit cards Frayer diagrams Graphic organizers Journal entries Guided observations Student indicators (for example, thumbs-up, thumbs-down, thumbs-sideways) Lab reports Student reflections on learning conditions
Summative (assessment of learning)	To determine degrees of student success/ mastery with designated goals at key points in a learning cycle and after considerable practice with designated outcomes. Used for the purpose of grading.	Performance assessments Student products Portfolios Public exhibitions Essays Tests

clues that become the connecting points for building larger cognitive and skill networks in the brain through the new learning.

- Virtually any work students do that is focused on the knowledge, understanding, and skills designated as essential for a segment of learning can be a formative assessment. The effective use of formative assessment does not so much mean creating a new bank of tests, activities, or projects. Rather, it means looking at what students do in the course of instruction with an eye toward understanding their current learning status and using the findings to plan instruction that will move all students forward.

- Effective preassessments, formative assessments, and summative assessments make room for student variance by providing multiple means of representation, multiple means of expression, and multiple means of engagement. Examples of providing multiple means of representation would be using both words and pictures in directions, writing or recording directions in a student's first language, or varying vocabulary and sentence structure based on a student's degree of language sophistication. Examples of providing multiple means of expression would be allowing students to express what they know through a diagram, storyboards, or an oral presentation. Examples of providing multiple means of engagement would be ensuring that assessment elements connect with students' experiences or reducing distractions in a testing situation for a student whose attention is easily diverted (CAST, 2008). Although the criteria for success on the assessment will generally stay the same for all students (other than those with individual educational plans specifying different goals and criteria), the formats, directions, and working conditions can vary as needed to ensure that a full range of students has ample opportunity to express critical knowledge, understanding, and skills (Tomlinson & McTighe, 2006).

- Providing feedback rather than grades for formative assessments ensures that students who struggle with the content have adequate practice time before their work is judged. This strategy helps them maintain optimism in the face of challenge and engage more fully with the work at hand. The same practice helps advanced learners by encouraging them to accept challenge without the fear of lowering their grades or losing their status as high achievers. It enables all students to develop a realistic sense that mistakes are a normal and instructive part of the learning process rather than academic sins to be avoided.

- Using assessment for learning increases student ownership of learning, student performance, and student learning efficacy. When students contribute to the construction of rubrics, set personal goals for learning or production, analyze their own work or the work of peers against rubrics or models, provide feedback to the teacher on what is working and not working for them in terms of both instruction and assessment, and reflect in meaningful ways on their own academic progress, learning becomes more satisfying and the learner more empowered.

A football coaching analogy is useful in thinking about assessment in a differentiated classroom. The coach's job is to prepare the team to win the next game. To do that, he must be quite clear on how the opposing team plays and what skills will be necessary to defeat it. Although winning the game is a team endeavor, a worthy coach would never just coach the team as a whole. Instead, he studies or assesses each player and provides feedback on what particular players must do to maximize their strengths in light of the upcoming challenge. There are clearly times when the coach instructs the entire team, but he would never say to the group, "On average, you're looking pretty good, so we can go home now." Only when every team member is playing to his full potential can the assessment and feedback loop subside. In the meantime, assessment guides the coach's development of both individual and team practice regimens, and specific, personalized feedback provides each player with the information necessary to build up to his best possible game.

Grading and Differentiation

Sometimes educators use the terms *grading* and *assessment* as if they were synonyms. They are not. Assessment, as this chapter explains, is a process that should begin as each unit of study begins, if not before. It should be a persistent part of instruction throughout the unit. For most of that time, assessment is diagnostic and formative, and its purpose is to guide teachers and students in working better and smarter. At key wrap-up points in the unit, summative assessments enable teachers and students to see how their efforts have paid off.

Diagnostic assessments or preassessments should never be graded, because students have not yet had the opportunity to learn what those assessments measure. Formative assessments should rarely be graded, because they are part of practice, and it is not beneficial to penalize students for practice work. Summative assessments are graded. They should align precisely with stated goals and the work teachers and students have done in pursuit of those goals. They are an anticipated benchmarking opportunity and should provide a fair assessment of student knowledge, understanding, and skills—especially if they provide for student variance in expression, engagement, and so on, while holding the goals and criteria for success steady. At that point, then, teachers have a need to report to parents, students, and other interested parties on student status relative to established goals.

The Value of Report Card Grades

Reporting grades is a concluding step in a long process—a summary statement about student progress (O'Connor, 2007). Report cards should not dominate or govern the teaching/learning process but rather should reflect it. Even then, teachers, students, and parents should understand that a report card is more like a physical exam than like an autopsy (Reeves, 2000). In other words, a report card provides a snapshot of a person who is still developing. It is never as multidimensional as the student is, nor is it the final word on the student's journey as a learner.

A report card grade should not come as a surprise to the student. Of course, the grade can be no more trustworthy than what led up to it. Students will understand and have regard for the report card grade if a teacher:

- Has a growth mindset

- Establishes a positive learning environment

- Has learning goals that are focused on understanding

- Communicates those learning goals clearly to students

- Teaches with those goals at the center of instruction

- Uses effective classroom assessment practices to inform both student and teacher work

- Modifies instructional plans to address gaps between students' current learning status and essential goals

Grades stemming from a classroom in which those practices are absent are (rightfully) less likely to get respect from students.

The following practices, some of which will sound familiar, lead to valid and reliable report card grades (National Research Council, 2001; O'Connor, 2007, 2009; Tomlinson & McTighe, 2006):

- Grades and report cards should be based on clearly specified learning goals known to both student and teacher throughout a unit of study, learning cycle, or marking period. Grading should not compare students to one another but rather should reveal the status of each student in relation to established learning goals.

- The evidence used for grades should be directly related to the specified learning goals. It lessens the validity of grades, for example, if students lose points for not putting a name on a paper or failing to bring a textbook to class.

- Not all student work should count toward a grade. Recall that formative assessment should rarely count in a final grade. The same is true for virtually all student practice work—including homework.

Practice that feels safe to students contributes dramatically to learner success.

- Assessments that contribute to grades and instruction leading up to grades should provide for student learning differences while holding constant required goals and criteria for success with those goals. This maximizes the likelihood of success for each student.

- Grades that occur late in a learning cycle should generally be emphasized more than grades occurring earlier in the cycle. By emphasizing more recent evidence, we acknowledge not only the importance of student persistence but also the impact of good teaching.

- Report cards should report achievement separately from other factors. When a report card grade is an average of attendance, classroom attitude, and assorted other elements, it is impossible for anyone to know what the student really knows, understands, and can do. In a differentiated classroom (if not all classrooms), it makes good sense to report three *separate* and interrelated grades. One would be a *performance* grade, a specific statement about the student's status relative to stated goals. A second would be a grade for the student's *habits of mind and work*. Does the student persist in the face of difficulty, ask for help when it is needed, look at issues from varied perspectives, set and work toward goals for improvement, complete assignments, and so on? These are characteristics of successful people in almost any field. They are also critical elements in a growth mindset. The third grade would reflect student *progress*. Given where the student began the marking period in relation to the established learning goals, how far has the student advanced? The three grades create an important loop, and its message is central to effective teaching as well as to grading. The teacher's message is "If you work in intelligent ways, you will grow academically. In time, it's highly likely that you will both achieve and surpass established expectations."

The Importance of Clear Goals

Throughout this chapter, as well as in other sections of the book, we continually emphasize how important it is for students to have a clear picture of the teacher's learning goals and of how they mesh with their personal goals. Not only does it make intuitive sense that we are more likely to embrace learning goals that are compatible with our own goals, but apparently our brain is wired to facilitate that embrace.

Success in learning something new is closely linked to a person's intentions regarding that learning. So researchers have used imaging studies to examine how the brain processes and acts on intentions. In a study using functional magnetic resonance imaging (fMRI), researchers found that when a subject was faced with a learning task, one specific brain region processed the learner's intentions shortly before another area decided whether to execute the task. Figure 4.2 shows where these two areas are located. After numerous trials, the researchers also noted that subjects more quickly completed tasks that appeared consistent with their intentions (Haynes et al., 2007). Other studies have found that intentions also affect attention to a learning task (Lau, Rogers, Haggard, & Passingham, 2004), as well as decisions about which task to execute when faced with a choice (Forstmann, Brass, Koch, & von Cramon, 2006). Students, then, are more likely to accept and perform better on those formative and summative assessments that are aligned with goals that were clearly defined throughout the learning experience.

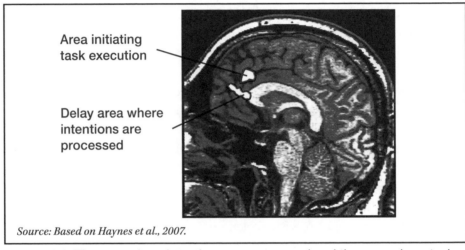

Area initiating
task execution

Delay area where
intentions are
processed

Source: Based on Haynes et al., 2007.

Figure 4.2: The area where intentions are processed and the area where task execution is initiated.

Rightly viewed, assessment is a facilitator of high levels of achievement for each student. It helps students learn and succeed by making as clear as possible the nature of their accomplishments and the progress of their learning at numerous points in the learning process (National Research Council, 2001). It helps teachers support the learning of individual students who inevitably vary as learners. It provides the insights needed for students not only to master specified content but also to develop as competent and motivated learners. At designated times, grades provide a shorthand to communicate clearly a summative statement about a particular student's work at a particular juncture in his or her life. Both effective classroom assessment and effective grading practices—like all aspects of quality teaching—require a high level of professional judgment and care to ensure that whatever is done promotes student learning.

A Better Scenario

Darius is feeling more confident this year, and his grades are better. He still struggles to find quiet time to do schoolwork at home, but it feels worth the effort now. Most of his teachers make learning goals clear to students at the outset of a unit. What happens in class seems to line up better with those goals. The teachers consistently work with students individually and as a class to set learning goals and monitor their progress toward those goals. The students get feedback on much of their work that helps them see what they are doing well and where they need extra work. Sometimes the students critique their own work or the work of classmates using rubrics they designed in collaboration with the teacher.

Darius has a better sense of what to study for when graded assessments occur, and he also likes the fact that several of his teachers give students two or three options for how they can show what they know. It is encouraging to him that his teachers have explained that a final assessment shows what he has learned for the entire unit or marking period. Therefore, if he shows mastery of content that was less clear to him earlier, the final grade overrides the earlier one. Darius feels that he is getting better at seeing what it means to be a successful learner. Most importantly, he knows he has the capacity to succeed. His effort is taking him where he wants to go.

Exercise 4.1

Questions for Teachers to Ask to Determine Whether an Assessment Is Effective

After reviewing a particular assessment, respond to the following questions. Then review your responses and reflect on whether you should consider making any changes to the assessments you use in class in order to more effectively meet the needs of a diverse group of students. Building administrators can use this activity at a faculty meeting to discuss the school's progress in using ongoing assessment data both as the teachers' entry point for differentiation and as a means of helping students understand and assume increasing responsibility for their success as learners.

1. Does the assessment clearly measure the learning objective that the students need to achieve?

2. Is the assessment measuring something that the students expect to be measured, or will it come as a surprise?

3. Is this the right type of assessment to use to measure this learning objective?

4. Does the assessment measure a fair representation of the components of the learning objective rather than your own favorite components?

5. Does the assessment measure the most important components of the learning objective rather than immaterial or tangential components?

6. Is the assessment appropriate for all the students who will use it?

page 1 of 2

7. Does the assessment make clear what students must do to provide a high-quality response?

8. Will the results of the assessment provide you with the information you need to determine how to refine and revise your instructional plans for the near term?

9. Will the results of the assessment provide students with the information they need to see where they are proficient and where they need to improve?

Possible Changes to Consider

CHAPTER 5

Differentiating in Response to Student Readiness

A basic educational principle is that new learning has to be based on old learning, on prior experiences and existing skills. Although this principle is known and agreed upon by all educators, in practice it is often overshadowed in schools by the administrative convenience of the linear curriculum and the single textbook. Homogeneous curricula and materials are problematic enough if all learners are from a single language and cultural background, but they are indefensible given the great diversity in today's classrooms, which requires a different conception of curricula and a different approach to materials. Differentiation and individualization are not a luxury in this context. They're a necessity.

—Aida Walqui, *Access and Engagement*

The term *readiness* refers to an individual's current proximity to, or proficiency with, a specific set of knowledge, understanding, and skills designated as essential to a particular segment of study. For example, if a second-grader is expected to be able to write a coherent paragraph with a main idea and related details, a student who cannot yet write a complete sentence is not ready to write paragraphs. By contrast, a classroom peer who loves writing and keeps a notebook of stories she writes in her spare time comes to the task of writing a coherent paragraph at a very advanced level of readiness. In fact, her level of readiness suggests that the task might be pointless for her because it will probably not extend her capacity as a writer. Said another way, teachers who pay attention to the variance in students' readiness levels ask themselves the question "What is the degree of match between the student's current level of knowledge, understanding, and skills and what he or she will be asked to do today (or this week, or in this unit)?"

Many factors affect a student's readiness to learn particular content at a particular time. A student's past school experiences, home opportunities, support systems, emotional state, and personal strengths and weaknesses are a few of the factors that can propel a student forward or hold a student back in regard to learning. These factors may be beyond the teacher's control at a given moment, but with a clear sense of where the student is in a learning sequence, the teacher can nonetheless take action to help the student move ahead. When a teacher does not attend to students' readiness needs, the likelihood of strong student outcomes decreases.

A Case in Point

Ann had been a good—if not great—mathematics student in elementary school. She didn't have to work especially hard to make strong grades in math. She watched what the teacher did, and it just somehow made sense. In middle school, however, she encountered algebra—or, more to the point, she encountered Mrs. Farr, who taught algebra with a vengeance. For long spans of time each day in class, Mrs. Farr stood at the chalkboard and wrote and solved algebra problems. She seemed to converse with the board more than with the students, erasing her work with one hand as she began a new problem with the other. However, from time to time, she did turn to the class and say, "Got that?" Ann did not get it, but she was shy and would never have said she didn't understand. To make matters worse, some of her friends nodded in the affirmative to the teacher's query.

Day by day, Ann got further behind in algebra, as each new skill was supposed to lead to the next one. In addition to feeling lost in the content, Ann lost her self-confidence as a math student and rapidly began to see herself as someone who was not good in math. Despite years of trying to dig out from the math content deficit, she never really regained either her former performance level in math or her sense that she could be competent in it.

Readiness Versus Ability

Readiness is *not* a synonym for *ability*. A student who appears to have limited ability in verbal areas might exhibit advanced readiness in vocabulary and knowledge related to the Civil War because he and his father participate in Civil War reenactments several times a year. By contrast, a student whose standardized test scores suggest strong verbal ability may struggle with oral production (that is, exhibit low readiness in that area) in Spanish class both because she does not hear new sounds as well as she retains what she reads and because she is shy and afraid of speaking aloud in a new language.

Distinguishing between readiness and ability is important for both teacher and student in terms of mindset about learning. Ability seems static—difficult to change—to many people. Although the truth is that ability is quite malleable, our tendency to see it as more permanent leads to a fixed mindset if we believe that ability will determine academic success. Readiness, however, changes from topic to topic, skill to skill. Further, although it is difficult for teachers to figure out how they might modify a student's ability, the strategies for addressing readiness needs should be quite evident. On a continuum of writing skills, for example, if a student cannot write a sentence and needs to write a paragraph, the teacher should be able to conclude that the student will need additional instruction, modeling, practice, and support in writing sentences so that he can move ahead to paragraph writing. If a student is already writing extensive, quality prose, it would be wise to help that student continue to develop her use of figurative language, transitions, characterization, or other more advanced skills that would move her along as a young writer.

Teachers looking for students' readiness needs in regard to specific academic content rather than focusing on students' ability are well positioned to work from a fluid or a growth mindset. As a result, it is likely that their students will also develop or continue to function with a fluid mindset. For them, too, it is clear that there are specific next steps that will result in progress toward or beyond specific goals. Success will seem less like an act of birth than an act of will.

> Teachers looking for students' readiness needs in specific content rather than focusing on students' ability are working from a growth mindset.

Why Addressing Readiness Matters

For decades, psychologists have explained that human beings learn when whatever they bring to a task in the way of context—knowledge, skill, understanding, experience—makes the task attainable for them. Lev Vygotsky (1978) explained the need for student/task match in terms of the zone of proximal development (ZPD). According to this theory, to maximize learning, a task should be a little beyond the learners' current reach, and the students should have a social support system (teacher, peers, and other knowledgeable people) to scaffold their work and help them bridge the gap between what they can do at the outset of the task and what they need to be able to do as a result of the task. A teacher who differentiates in response to students' readiness variance uses readiness-based assessment information to create tasks that are a little too hard for particular students and to establish the support systems necessary to help them move forward to a new level of competence and confidence. In time, the students will become less dependent on the scaffolding and will be able to work with the particular content effectively enough to get themselves "unstuck" when necessary. Ultimately, using the content becomes natural to the students. At that point, task difficulty must escalate for new learning to occur. When students can complete a task with no "stretch," they may receive a good grade for their work, but they will not grow as learners. Neither will students learn when a task is well beyond their reach. Figure 5.1 (page 88) illustrates the stages of learning in a recursive zone of proximal development model.

The concept of ZPD has been used for years in the field of reading to determine materials that are appropriate for a student's current reading skills. If a book,

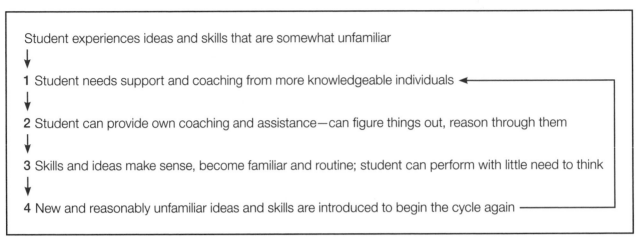

Student experiences ideas and skills that are somewhat unfamiliar

1 Student needs support and coaching from more knowledgeable individuals

2 Student can provide own coaching and assistance—can figure things out, reason through them

3 Skills and ideas make sense, become familiar and routine; student can perform with little need to think

4 New and reasonably unfamiliar ideas and skills are introduced to begin the cycle again

Figure 5.1: The zone of proximal development model.

for example, is at an "independent level" for a student, he or she can read the book easily. It may be a good book for pleasure reading, but it will not move the student forward in vocabulary acquisition. A book at the student's "instructional level" will require some support from a teacher or a peer who is a more skilled reader in order for the student to comprehend the text, but at this level, with effective support, the student will grow as a reader. A book at a "frustration level" for the student, will, as the label suggests, be too difficult for the student to handle until he or she has developed additional vocabulary and reading skills. The goal with reading, as it should be in other content areas, is to ensure that a student most often works at an "instructional level" with scaffolding. In time, skills that were once at a student's independent level and those that were once at a frustration level will be at the student's instructional level. In other words, only when teachers can match tasks to a student's current point of readiness, provide support for learning, ensure appropriate practice for mastery, and then introduce new content will the student really learn.

The Challenge of ZPD in the Classroom

The challenge, of course, in virtually every classroom is that, for any given segment of content, students will be at various ZPD points. If a teacher attempts to teach knowledge, understanding, and skills as though everyone in the class were at the same point of readiness—that is, in the same zone of proximal development—it is likely that some students will be in the "learning stage" while others are coasting and still others are confused and frustrated.

Research in cognitive psychology over an extended period of time indicates that students across the achievement spectrum learn better and feel better about themselves when teachers diagnose their current skill levels and prescribe tasks appropriate for their points of readiness (Csikszentmihalyi, Rathunde, & Whalen, 1993; Fisher et al., 1980; Hunt, 1971). In addition, a number of studies have found that students in nongraded and multi-age classrooms—where attention to readiness differences is the norm—generally achieve better than peers in single-grade classrooms and develop stronger study habits, better collaborative skills, and more positive attitudes about school (Anderson & Pavan, 1993; Fisher et al., 1980; Gayfer, 1991; Miller, 1990).

It is helpful to note that Vygotsky talked about learning "zones" rather than learning "points." In other words, it's not necessary to know a student's exact status in regard to the degree of task difficulty. Rather, the teacher can look for evidence that tasks are so difficult that a student is frustrated and cannot proceed, or that a student needs a bit more practice, or that the task is about right for a student, or that a student completes a task with little or no effort and therefore is likely underchallenged. Teachers arrive at these sorts of judgments by observing students while they work and taking quick notes on what they see, knowing a student's status with reading and academic vocabulary, being aware of a student's general independence as a learner, looking carefully at preassessment and formative assessment information, and making a note of student responses during discussions. It is also very important for teachers to ask students how they are feeling about the challenge level of their work. Understanding a student's learning zone for a particular topic and content area is critical for readiness differentiation.

One word of caution, however: there are many students who, for various reasons, may struggle with fundamental skills but who understand content accurately and are keen thinkers. Such students may well need scaffolding for reading, writing, following directions, and so on, but be able to work with complex ideas as long as that scaffolding is available. Do not allow one indicator (for example, test scores or oral participation in class) to skew your understanding of a student's capacity to make sense of, apply, or transfer knowledge.

Support From Neuroscience

Neuroscientific studies over the past decades that have looked at the dynamics of the brain's attention systems lend support to Vygotsky's basic ideas about the ZPD. Because the brain's main job is to help its owner survive, any new (novel) stimulus from the environment is likely to catch its attention. Specialized structures in the midbrain respond to the stimulus and alert the frontal lobe—the brain's executive control center (see fig. 5.2, page 90). The brain needs to evaluate the stimulus to determine whether it poses a threat and, if so, decide what action is appropriate—fight or flight, for example. Many stimuli, of course, are not life threatening, but some may cause stress nevertheless. A learning assignment that students perceive as too difficult (that is, outside their ZPD) will often produce stress because students fear failure or, at the very least, do not want to appear incompetent in front of their peers.

One revealing study using fMRI showed that the midbrain structures that respond to novelty are associated with neighboring structures that play

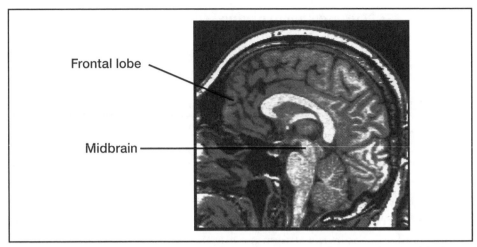

Figure 5.2: The area of the midbrain whose structures communicate with the frontal lobe.

a role in reward processing (Wittmann, Bunzeck, Dolan, & Düzel, 2007). When the study subjects had to process information related to novel images, both the novelty regions and the reward-processing areas were stimulated. Furthermore, the hippocampus—that part of the brain responsible for encoding memories—was also activated. These areas are heavily populated with neurons that produce dopamine, a neurotransmitter associated with pleasurable experiences. Whenever we participate in activities that result in a release of dopamine, the brain responds not only with pleasure but also with increased focus, memory, and motivation (Storm & Tecott, 2005). Designers of computer games are very much aware of this dopamine-reward system. As players progress toward achieving the game's objective, they feel the pleasure of the dopamine reward. This keeps them intrinsically motivated to persevere through the game's more difficult levels of challenge (Gee, 2007).

These findings lead to speculation that the brain may turn its attention to novel learning activities because it perceives a potential reward in doing so and that it may encode the experience in memory. It follows, then, that students who believe they can accomplish a learning task (that is, the task lies within their ZPD) are likely to attempt it and remember it. A task that is perceived as too easy (that is, outside their ZPD) will be identified by the hippocampal memory system as having already been accomplished and thus as offering no novelty (Kumaran & Maguire, 2007). Moreover, if the student finds no meaning in the task, the brain is not likely even to orient itself to the task, let alone activate its novelty and memory areas (Friedman, Goldman, Stern, & Brown, 2009).

> The brain may turn its attention to novel learning activities because it perceives a potential reward.

Building Bridges

When teachers differentiate for readiness, their goal for instructing some students is to build a bridge that will enable those students to move beyond deficits from ineffective prior learning experiences and to progress to mastery of the currently required content. For students who already demonstrate competence with required content, the goal is to build bridges to substantive advanced learning so that they can continue their development. For many students, readiness differentiation will require something less ambitious than bridge building. It will be a kind of fine-tuning—a little more time to work on this task, a mini-lesson to clarify a point of confusion, a book or website that is a little more sophisticated, and so on—so that they can develop a sound footing with what they are asked to learn.

The Role of Classroom Elements in Planning for Readiness Differentiation

The interdependence of classroom elements is clear when a teacher begins to make plans for addressing varied learner needs. Learning environment, curriculum, assessment, classroom management, and instruction (differentiation) are tightly connected, and reflecting on those connections is an important part of the planning process. Figure 5.3 depicts some ways in which the elements are interdependent when a teacher plans for and implements differentiation.

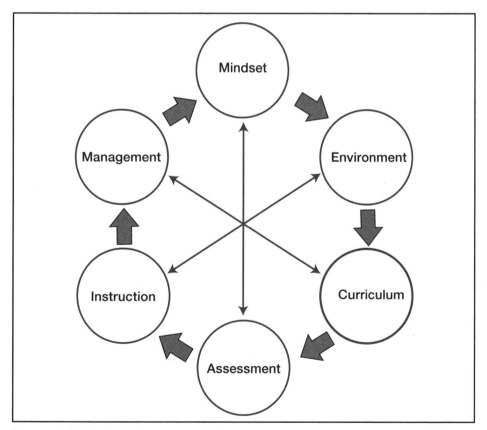

Figure 5.3: The interdependence of classroom elements that shape readiness differentiation.

The Learning Environment

It is impossible for a student to feel safe, supported, and affirmed in a classroom where work is consistently too hard or too easy. Therefore, adapting instruction to attend to readiness has a positive impact on the students' sense that the teacher understands and cares about them and wants them to succeed. Knowing that the teacher believes that everyone in the class is important and intends for each student to succeed leads students to respect their classmates and gives them the feeling of belonging to a team or a "community of learners."

Curriculum

Curriculum, of course, provides the teaching/learning destination for planning. In terms of readiness differentiation, the curriculum should make clear what students should know (K), understand (U), and be able to do (D) as a result of a unit of study. In that way, the curriculum signals the teacher about common goals. The teacher, however, will have to figure out (hopefully with the assistance of colleagues and professional materials) what a *continuum* of knowledge, understanding, and skills would look like around the common KUDs. In other words, if a student is not currently ready to handle a prescribed skill, what steps in mastery would he likely have to move through to arrive at the desired level of competency? If a student is weak in the foundational academic vocabulary of a subject, what are the essential terms she must master to build toward competence with the currently required, and more advanced, vocabulary? If a student already demonstrates proficiency with the understandings or principles related to a current unit on electricity, for instance, what are the next steps in exploring, extending, and applying those principles? The prescribed curriculum does not exist in a vacuum; it is part of a larger network of knowledge, understanding, and skills that came before it and that will continue afterward. Having a clear sense of both the prescribed content *and* its larger context prepares a teacher to make effective readiness adaptations.

Assessment

Assessment data, of course, provide much of the information on which a teacher bases decisions about readiness adaptations for particular students. Both preassessments and formative assessments must be tightly aligned with what the unit framework indicates students must know, understand, and be able to do as a result of studying the unit. Preassessment of readiness gives a teacher advance warning about student status relative to key knowledge, understanding, and skills—including any gaps students may have in the prerequisite KUDs. Armed with that information, the teacher can make targeted readiness adjustments very early in a unit so as to curb an accumulating deficit of proficiency and confidence for some students and to avoid pointless work and reinforcement of ineffective work habits for others.

Formative assessment—also tightly aligned with unit KUDs—should provide the teacher with frequent, fresh insights into the degree to which each student is progressing as necessary for successful outcomes. Again, ongoing or formative assessment data should guide a teacher's instructional planning for readiness. When a student also understands that the purpose of ongoing assessment is to support success rather than to judge, and when the student is able to examine her progress toward clear goals, she is a more encouraged learner, and the classroom environment reflects for her the appropriate balance of safety, challenge, and support.

Informed by current assessment information aligned with essential KUDs, a teacher can make astute instructional plans targeted to students' varied readiness needs. These plans may involve but not be limited to:

- Using small-group instruction with students who have similar needs with regard to skills

- Using more complex or more straightforward task directions for some students

- Assigning differentiated homework

- Using materials at multiple reading levels

- Using instructional strategies such as tiering or learning contracts

- Providing supports for students who have difficulty reading

- Frontloading or preteaching key academic vocabulary to students with weak subject-specific vocabulary

- Assigning varied work at skills centers

Occasionally, it is important to form heterogeneous rather than homogeneous readiness groups so that students can learn from one another and can see themselves in varied contexts.

Classroom Management

Differentiated instruction means that students in the same classroom will be working with different tasks or materials some of the time. If students are to function comfortably and effectively in such a classroom system, the teacher must work with them to establish flexible classroom routines. This collaborative process helps students understand the teacher's thinking more fully, feel a sense of ownership in the classroom, achieve success more readily, and build a sense of teamwork or partnership in the classroom. To make it possible for the teacher to target students' varying readiness needs, students must understand how to move around the classroom appropriately (and when it is not appropriate to do so), how to find materials they need, how to work without hindering the work of others, how to get and give help when the teacher is working with other students, how to keep track of their own work, and so on. Flexible classroom management makes differentiated instruction possible, enhances the likelihood that each student will succeed with important curriculum goals, and creates a hospitable learning environment that makes room for all different kinds of learners. The specifics of managing a differentiated classroom will be explored in chapter 8.

Instruction

With high-quality curriculum, plans for assessment to inform instruction, and effective, flexible classroom routines in place, the groundwork is laid for instruction that is attentive to the variety of needs in the classroom. Certainly there will be times throughout a unit of study when it makes good sense for the class to work as a whole group. There will be many other times, however, when it is important to address student differences in readiness, interest, or learning profile to ensure student success. That is when instruction—the fifth classroom element—takes center stage. At that point, teachers use what they are learning from ongoing assessment to provide varied avenues for students to master essential content. Most of the remainder of this chapter focuses on guidelines and strategies for differentiating instruction in response to students' readiness levels.

Some Guidelines for Differentiating in Response to Student Readiness

The decisions that teachers make to respond to students' inevitable variance in readiness, like all important teacher decisions, should be systematic and grounded in what we know about effective teaching and successful learning. The following guidelines should serve as reminders that addressing student readiness needs is a part of good teaching, not an extra or an add-on.

- Identify and articulate in student language what students should know, understand, and be able to do as a result of the unit of study you will be differentiating. This information will give you and your students clarity about the destination everyone is expected to reach.

- Develop a preassessment that aligns with the essential KUDs and includes a check of prerequisite knowledge for the unit.

- Whatever grade level or subject you teach, be sure to do a preassessment of student readiness in reading, writing, and listening early in the school year, and perhaps at the midpoint of the year as well. Having students write a simple set of directions generally yields an adequate writing sample. Asking students to read a passage from the text and answer a comprehension question and then listen to you read a passage and answer a comprehension question is typically adequate to help you get a sense of who comprehends when they hear but not when they read, who comprehends when they read but not when they hear, who comprehends in both situations, and who does not function well in either. Even if you teach high school, you should consider using this readiness preassessment because some students at that level are struggling readers and poor listeners. If other skills are foundational to your grade and course, sample those as well.

- Administer your preassessment of unit KUDs and prerequisite knowledge several days before the start of the new unit so that you will have time to become familiar with what the preassessment shows about students' points of readiness for the unit.

- Based on preassessment information and other knowledge you have of your students, think about ways in which you can provide early support for students who will need to learn both backward (attend to content deficits) and forward (work toward current goals). Find as much time as possible for those students to do guided and supported work that will help them gain academic ground rather than continue a backward slide.

- Based on preassessment information and other knowledge you have of your students, think about ways in which you can meaningfully move ahead those students who already show mastery of most of the unit's content goals. Consider longer-term assignments and tasks that will allow the advanced students to work for depth and quality in fewer areas rather than churn out many smaller and less substantial assignments.

- Look for key points in the unit when your experience tells you that students may develop misunderstandings, begin to get ahead or behind with important skills, find that the text and supplementary materials are too hard or too easy, and so on.

- Incorporate strategies into your instructional design that address readiness needs at those key points. For example, for English learners, you can plan to supply relevant materials in the students' first language that they can read before reading key English materials. You can use learning contracts or learning menus that allow targeted assignments based on a student's particular needs, provide reading digests of texts for students who find reading the text too demanding, and use demonstrations to make abstract ideas more accessible to students. Be sure that students regularly have reading materials matched to their reading readiness levels. Many such approaches to readiness differentiation require only modest time for planning and make good use of class time as well. They need not be laborious for the teacher but will serve students well.

- Plan for flexible grouping. First, determine points at which it will be critical to have students work in like-readiness pairs or groups. Then build in times for mixed-readiness pairs or groups to work together. These groups may be especially useful in brainstorming for ideas and reviewing key content. Next, plan for groups based on student interest and learning profile.

- Remember that most students have to be taught to make judicious readiness decisions for themselves. Therefore, when students self-select a readiness group or a task level, give them criteria for making the choice, evidence on which they can base their choice, and debriefing opportunities to reflect on the appropriateness of the choice. To the degree that students are not prepared to make thoughtful readiness choices, don't hesitate to take on the important role of diagnostician and prescriber.

- Think about classroom procedures and routines that will need to be in place for the differentiated tasks to work as they should. Then make sure the students are ready to participate successfully in those routines. (See chapter 8.)

- As students work independently and in small groups, use your time to meet with small groups of students and to move around the classroom monitoring student progress, talking with students individually, and jotting down quick notes about what you observe. This monitoring process provides important instructional opportunities and contributes to your general understanding of students and their progress.

- Use formative assessments (including student activities) at frequent intervals throughout the unit to follow the students' growth in essential knowledge, understanding, and skills. Use what you learn to shape instructional plans in the next day or two.

- Be sure that student activities align tightly with the unit's essential knowledge, understanding, and skills. Look at most activities as opportunities for student practice and as formative assessments rather than as graded pieces. Study student work to understand learning needs and growth patterns. Involve the students in the examination of their work based on pre-established criteria for success so that they become increasingly able to make wise learning choices on their own behalf and increasingly aware of the direct link between their effort and their success.

- Plan up. There will be times when students need to focus on increasing their proficiency with skills, and times when they need to rehearse and clarify knowledge. Be sure, however, that all students have work that focuses on understanding how the content makes sense, how people use it in the world, and how it relates to their lives. You will need to provide additional scaffolding for some students to apply, analyze, support, and critique ideas and to transfer key content. But understanding is possible for virtually all students, and learning is more purposeful and durable when students make meaning of what they learn.

- Do *not* envision readiness differentiation as giving some students more work and others less work. It is seldom useful for students to do only half of what they do not understand and seldom useful or motivating for students to do more of what they have already mastered. Differentiating *skills* based on student readiness is a matter of finding a student's current point of performance along a continuum of skills and supporting the student's movement up the continuum. Differentiating *knowledge* based on readiness is a matter of understanding what knowledge about a given topic is foundational, what is essential, and what is more sophisticated and—again—helping a student work from his or her current point toward increasingly advanced knowledge. Differentiating *understandings* based on readiness means helping students work along a continuum of tasks and applications that deal with the understanding in a more foundational, concrete, single-faceted, highly scaffolded way to tasks and applications that require increasing degrees of abstractness, unfamiliarity, multifacetedness, open-endedness, and so on. (See the section on tiering later in this chapter for additional information about differentiating understandings based on readiness.) In the end, planning up means ensuring that virtually all students will use the knowledge and skills they are mastering to explore and extend their understanding.

- Because emotions play such a key role in attention, seek input from students on how they are feeling about their proficiency with key content, and ask them to suggest ways that teaching and learning plans could be modified to benefit their growth.

- Keep studying your content to understand more and more fully how it is organized to make sense, how you can engage students with its "stories," and which knowledge, understandings, and skills are truly essential to the discipline it represents. Keep studying your students so that it becomes increasingly clear to you where they progress smoothly, where they get tangled up, and what you can do to connect them effectively and efficiently with what matters most in a subject.

Exercise 5.1 (page 106) provides a checklist for reflecting on teacher practice in addressing student readiness.

Differentiating Content, Process, and Product Based on Student Readiness

It is useful to consider how three key curriculum elements can be differentiated based on student readiness needs. These elements are content, process, and product. They are a part of all classrooms—whether we are conscious of them or not. Thinking about differentiating these three elements extends the likelihood that a teacher will consider a wide range of options for supporting the growth of students at a wide range of readiness levels.

Content

Content is what we plan to teach, what we want students to learn. It includes what we want students to know, understand, and be able to do, as well as the narratives, events, and examples that make up a unit or topic of study. There are two ways to think about differentiating content. First, teachers can differentiate the actual "stuff"—the Ks, Us, and Ds. Second, teachers can differentiate how students get access to the stuff. The fact that we want all students to work with the same KUDs would seem to indicate that the preferable—or at least more often-used approach—is to differentiate how students get access to the stuff or the content. For example, a teacher may put a book on tape so that students who have great difficulty reading text can hear the material rather than read it.

To differentiate access, a teacher might do the following:

- Use video images to augment complex text.

- Offer demonstrations during a lecture so that students can see a concrete application of an abstract idea.

- Sit with a small group of English learners and summarize key ideas for them before they begin the day's task.

- Bookmark a university website for two students who are advanced on a topic and would benefit more from an expert-level discussion of the topic than from reading about it in a grade-level text.

- Provide a partially completed matrix for students who have difficulty with attention so that they can more readily take notes during a presentation.

There are, as noted earlier, times when it makes sense to actually differentiate the stuff rather than only the modes of accessing the stuff. A seventh-grader who spells on a second-grade level will not benefit from a seventh-grade spelling list at the outset of the year. Spelling patterns build over time, and if the student is lacking in third- through sixth-grade patterns, working with the seventh-grade spelling words will be about as effective as trying to memorize a phone book in another language. The student will fare better by working intensely with a second-grade list and moving as quickly as possible toward readiness for later lists. A student who knows an immense amount about Greek and Roman mythology will benefit more from reading the myths of other cultures than from simply reviewing what he has known for years. The student who is supposed to learn to multiply fractions this year but has never learned to multiply will need to have multiplication as part of her KUDs. There is little hope that she will master fractions otherwise.

Note, however, that it is not the case that students must continue to drill basic skills before they can consider advanced concepts. The idea that Bloom's Revised Taxonomy, for example, is a ladder students must climb rung by rung to the top is incorrect and unnecessarily consigns many students to low-level curriculum more or less permanently (Tomlinson & McTighe, 2006). Of course, basic knowledge and understanding must be in place. But in many cases, teachers can help students learn to apply more fundamental skills and concepts in rich and engaging contexts or can help students master foundational concepts through individual and small-group work, at centers, with targeted homework, in mini-lessons, and so on, even as the students move ahead with more advanced work.

Process

Process begins when students stop taking in information and begin to work actively with it. Process is often called "activities" in school. A better term for it is "sense-making activities." Process is how students come to own what they should know, understand, and can do. When process begins, students stop "borrowing" information from other sources and make it their own. In other words, this is the point when a student tries out ideas, compares them with what she already knows, and applies them to new settings. Activities can focus on knowledge, understanding, or skills but are most powerful when they call on students to integrate them. Among the many ways to differentiate process based on readiness are the following:

- Increase or decrease the complexity of the task while holding steady the desired outcomes.

- Increase or decrease the number of facets or variables in the task.

- Ask students to work with partners to solve a problem versus working alone.

- Provide additional models or other scaffolding to make a task accessible.

- Use expert-level rubrics to guide the work of highly able learners.

Product

Products are ways that students show what they have come to know, understand, and be able to do as the result of a long segment of study. The model of differentiation referenced in this book uses *product* as a synonym for a summative assessment. While more typical tests have a place as summative devices, they generally measure knowledge and skills. This model of differentiation encourages the use of more authentic performance tasks as summative measures or products because they call on students to demonstrate understanding and to transfer what they have learned to new contexts. Strategies for differentiating products based on student readiness might include the following:

- Provide more check-in dates for a student who has difficulty staying on track with lengthy tasks.

- Provide more-complex or less-complex resources for students based on their reading levels.

- Ask students to set personal goals for their products based on the next steps they need to take with skills as well as have common goals based on the unit's KUDs.

- Use community mentors to support the understanding of one student and to extend the understanding of another.

Exercise 5.2 (page 108) offers some additional examples of ways in which teachers might differentiate content, process, and product based on student readiness needs.

Differentiating With Learning Contracts and Tiering

This chapter contains numerous strategies for addressing student readiness. We will take a closer look here at two commonly used strategies: learning contracts and tiering.

Learning Contracts

Learning contracts take many forms, such as learning menus, learning tickets, learning agendas, and think-tac-toes. Whatever the form, when contracts and contract-like strategies are used to address variations in student readiness, they tend to have the following common elements:

- The teacher places work on a student's contract that (1) reflects the key knowledge, understanding, and/or skills for a particular unit or topic and (2) focuses on the student's areas of greatest need. Sometimes contracts also emphasize or link to student strengths.

- Formative assessment data guide the teacher in choosing items for students.

- Students' contracts typically look very much alike—same format, same number of required items—but the items themselves differ. Some of the items are shared by most or all students, and some are shared by only a few students.

- The contract may include only required items or a combination of required items and choice options.

- Students have some freedom in selecting the order in which they will complete tasks on the contract. They may also have the freedom to decide where to sit in the room and which parts of the contract to do at home versus at school. If a student does not make effective use of the freedom, the teacher simply makes assignments for the student to support successful completion of the work.

- Each student keeps a planning chart indicating his or her plan to ensure that all of the work will be appropriately completed by a specified deadline. The chart is displayed on the student's desk for teacher review whenever the student is working on the contract.

- As the student completes each piece of work, he or she has it checked by the teacher or a designated "checker" to ensure accuracy and understanding. If a piece is not approved, the student must revise the work.

Contracts are helpful to the teacher because they allow practice targeted at a student's needs. They are attractive to students both because of the elements of choice and because they are typically a good fit for their readiness levels and therefore support their success—a very brain-friendly situation.

Figure 5.4 (page 102) shows a simple, hand-written contract that a teacher created for her first-grade class. The eight assignments on the contract, one in each segment of the circle, were designed to correspond to the particular math and literacy skills that she felt were most important for the students' growth at that time. All eight assignments were simultaneously available somewhere in the room. The contract in the figure has been filled out for a student named Katee. As Katee finished an item of work, her teacher reviewed it, recorded the date on which it was finished (which allowed the teacher to monitor Katee's pace of work completion), and gave it either a check (meaning satisfactory work) or a check-plus (high-quality work). If a piece did not merit at least a check, Katee had to work with it until it was satisfactory.

The boxes along the bottom of the chart contain options that Katee had if she finished her work early. To keep too many students from wanting to do the same bottom-of-the-page task at the same time, students could request other options that appealed to them. They also had a hole punched in the option box when they went to that center, and they could not return to the center once that choice was hole-punched. The teacher found that having her students work intensely for part of four class days on skills that reflected their particular needs increased achievement in those areas noticeably for most students.

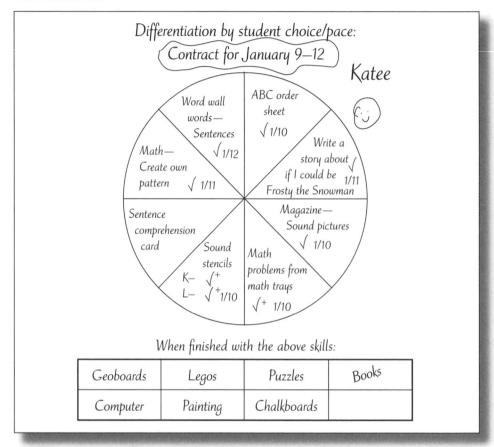

Differentiation by student choice/pace:
Contract for January 9–12

Katee

Word wall words— Sentences √ 1/12

ABC order sheet √ 1/10

Write a story about if I could be Frosty the Snowman √ 1/11

Math— Create own pattern √ 1/11

Magazine— Sound pictures √ 1/10

Sentence comprehension card

Sound stencils K– √+ L– √+ 1/10

Math problems from math trays √+ 1/10

When finished with the above skills:

Geoboards	Legos	Puzzles	Books
Computer	Painting	Chalkboards	

Figure 5.4: A first-grade mathematics and literacy contract.

Tiering

Tiering is a strategy that allows all students to work with the same content but at a degree of difficulty that provides an appropriate level of challenge. In other words, tiering allows students to work in their own zones of proximal development or in a state of moderate challenge while working toward common goals. Many kinds of student work can be tiered—for example, learning centers, journal prompts, products, problems, labs, homework, and assessments. Tiered tasks typically have the following characteristics:

■ All versions of the task focus on the same essential knowledge, understanding, and/or skills.

- All versions of the task require students to think or reason to complete the work.

- All versions of the task look equally interesting or inviting to students.

- The assignment of students to particular tiers is informed by ongoing assessment information and other observations of student readiness, although at some points, teachers find it advantageous to allow students to select their tiers themselves, based on their understanding of their own learning needs.

We offer two "In the Classroom" scenarios to show tiering in action. The first example is from a middle school science class. The teacher has created two versions of a task. At both tiers, students must think about what happened in an experiment as well as the meaning of what happened. At both tiers, students must communicate in clear language the significance of the experiment. Tier 2, however, is a bit more abstract, complex, and open-ended than Tier 1. It is better suited to students who already have a firm understanding of the content and who think more abstractly.

The primary-grade assignment in the second example has three tiers. Once again, the assignments reflect different degrees of difficulty in response to student need, but all students must consider characteristics of good friends.

In the Classroom
Reflecting on a Lab Experiment (Middle School)

Ms. Maeng, a middle school science teacher, wanted her students to reflect on a lab experiment they had just completed. She created a task with two tiers and gave each student a slip of paper that had one of the tiers on it. She asked all students to follow the reflection prompt carefully and to make sure that their work showed their best insight and understanding. The two tiers of the reflection prompt read as follows:

Tier 1
A classmate had to leave the room today just as the lab experiment was beginning to come to a conclusion. Please write that student a note explaining what happened in the lab, why it happened, and what practical use there is in the real world for what the experiment shows us. You are the student's only hope for clarity! Be as much help as possible.

Tier 2
Select a key or critical element in the experiment today. Change it in some way. What will happen in the experiment with that change? Why? What principle can you infer? Be sure you go for something useful, insightful, and intellectually or scientifically meaningful as your choice.

In the Classroom

Characteristics of a Good Friend (Primary Grades)

During a study of friendship in a primary class, Ms. Wu wanted her students to reflect on the characteristics of a good friend. Her students varied in their independence with language, but she wanted all of them to think about the same topic. She tiered the assignment to account for variance in language skill while asking each student to demonstrate an understanding of the attributes of friendship. All students had the same set of characteristics of good friends to guide their work. The teacher recorded directions for each tier of the assignment on small audio recorders so that students could hear them as they began their work.

Tier 1

Good friends listen to one another. They care about one another. They are happy when a friend is happy and sad when a friend is sad. They try to help one another when they can. They know they can trust one another. Draw a picture of friends that you think shows these characteristics of good friends. Cut out the words that tell characteristics of good friends. Paste them on your drawing to show how the friends you drew are good friends. Talk with people at your table about your ideas. Help one another be sure that your pictures show what it means to be a good friend.

Tier 2

Look at the two pictures in your folder. Decide which picture best shows the characteristics of good friends and which picture does not show the characteristics of a good friend. Use the word strips on your table to label the pictures. Make a check mark beside the word strip if the picture shows the way good friends would probably be. Make an X beside the word strip if the picture doesn't show the way good friends would probably be.

Tier 3

Look at the picture in your folder. Decide if the people in the picture are examples of good friends or not. Use the list of characteristics of good friends to help you think about the picture. Then write a letter to the people telling them whether you think they seem like good friends or not. Be sure to use the characteristics of good friends to help the people understand why you think they are good friends or why you think they are not good friends.

Figure 5.5 shows a useful tool that is intended to scaffold teacher thinking about what it means to create several versions (usually two to four) of a task for the purpose of having each student work at a level of moderate challenge. The tool is called the Equalizer and is designed to look like the slide controls on a CD player that allow a listener to adjust volume, tone, bass, and so on. Operating on the same principle, this tool allows a teacher who is creating various tiers of a task to adjust the difficulty of the versions. By mentally moving one or more sliders toward the left, the teacher can create a version of the task at a more basic level of difficulty, and by mentally moving one or more of the sliders toward the right, the teacher can create a version of the task at a more advanced level of difficulty. If we look again at the two "In the Classroom" scenarios, we can determine which elements on the Equalizer were probably used to vary the degree of difficulty of the middle school lab prompts and of the primary assignments on friendship.

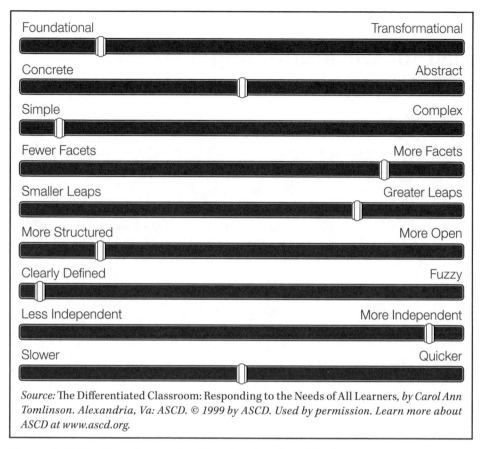

Source: The Differentiated Classroom: Responding to the Needs of All Learners, by Carol Ann Tomlinson. Alexandria, Va: ASCD. © 1999 by ASCD. Used by permission. Learn more about ASCD at www.ascd.org.

Figure 5.5: The Equalizer—a tool for planning tiered tasks.

A Better Scenario

Mrs. Farr preassessed her algebra students to uncover their weaknesses in prerequisite math skills. She also gave them a simple algebra problem to see how they would approach it, even though they had had no prior class work in algebra. She noticed that Ann's general math skills were strong but that she did not attempt the algebra problem. As Mrs. Farr began the year with her students, she explained that she would be monitoring their progress very frequently and would provide opportunities for them to get clarification when the new skills and ideas were unclear to them, as well as opportunities to try challenge tasks when they felt ready.

In addition to using frequent formative assessments, such as exit cards, Mrs. Farr often asked her students to indicate whether they felt ready to "race ahead," "take a practice drive," or "restart their engines" with regard to a particular skill or application. Based on assessment information and/or student indication, she provided tasks (including small-group work with the teacher) at different levels of complexity at least twice a week. She also provided differentiated homework and learning contracts to enable students to do work that would boost their current level of understanding and performance. She had her students participate in problem-solving triads, in which they solved a few problems together before soloing with similar problems at home.

Ann had heard that algebra was really hard, and she was afraid she might not be able to do it. In Mrs. Farr's class, however, it was hard to get behind! Ann tells other students that algebra isn't really as hard as people make it out to be.

Exercise 5.1

A Checklist for Differentiating Instruction Based on Student Readiness

Respond to the following questions. After you finish, review your responses and reflect on whether you should consider making any changes to your instruction to better meet your students' varied readiness needs. Building administrators can use this activity at a faculty meeting to discuss the school's progress in working toward differentiation in response to student readiness. The questions could also provide a framework for planning professional development and for helping teachers more fully incorporate differentiation based on student readiness into their instructional plans.

1. Do you understand the difference between readiness and ability?

2. Do you have clearly articulated KUDs for the lesson or unit?

3. Are students clear on the learning goals?

4. Do you have a preassessment clearly aligned with the KUDs?

5. Does the preassessment also check for prerequisite knowledge?

6. Have you done a check of student readiness in reading, writing, and other fundamental skills necessary for the topic?

7. Will you administer the preassessment far enough in advance of the unit to have time to plan based on what you learn about student readiness?

8. Have you made early plans to vigorously address deficits in fundamental skills, prerequisite skills, and KUDs?

9. Have you made early plans to extend the learning of students who demonstrate initial mastery of most or all of the essential KUDs?

10. Have you identified key points in the unit where students are likely to fall behind, develop misunderstandings, or move ahead rapidly?

Differentiation and the Brain • © 2011 Solution Tree Press • solution-tree.com

Visit **go.solution-tree.com/instruction** to download this page.

11. Have you built into the unit at those key points the use of instructional strategies and approaches that address readiness needs?

12. Have you planned for both homogeneous and heterogeneous readiness groups during the unit?

13. If students will select readiness tasks that match their needs, have you prepared them to make those choices wisely?

14. Have you developed classroom routines and procedures that support having students work with varied tasks and in varied group configurations?

15. Have you prepared students to work effectively with, and contribute to the refinement of, those routines and procedures?

16. Are you using student work time to meet with or teach small groups and to monitor student work and progress?

17. Will you use regular formative assessments (including student activities) to inform your instructional plans to address students' varied readiness needs?

18. Are differentiated activities tightly aligned with the unit's KUDs?

19. Are all students working with understandings that are developed and scaffolded for their readiness levels?

20. Are you consistently studying your content and students and reflecting on ways to connect each student with essential content at a readiness level that benefits the growth of the student?

Possible Changes to Consider

Exercise 5.2

Differentiating Content, Process, and Product Based on Student Readiness

Here are some suggestions for activities that can help you differentiate content, process, and product based on your students' readiness. Add to each section other activities that you and your colleagues feel are appropriate. Building administrators can use this activity at a faculty meeting to discuss the school's progress in working toward differentiating these three components based on student readiness.

Differentiating Content Based on Readiness

1. Use a metaphor from a student's life to help him or her understand an abstract idea in science.

2. Provide students with texts in which the most essential passages have been highlighted so that a student with reading/language difficulties can succeed with what matters most.

3. Use small-group instruction targeted at members' readiness levels.

4. Ask a student who is struggling with reading to meet with two reading groups a day rather than one.

5. Offer mini-workshops as students' work indicates difficulty with key content.

6. Provide key vocabulary lists with both drawn and written definitions to help students understand a text or lecture.

Additional Activities

Differentiating Process Based on Readiness

1. Use manipulatives to help some students understand fractions (but don't use them with students who already understand the concept fully).

2. Use a computer math tutorial that assesses a student's readiness and provides tasks and feedback at the appropriate level.

Differentiation and the Brain • © 2011 Solution Tree Press • solution-tree.com

Visit **go.solution-tree.com/instruction** to download this page.

3. Assign students to learning stations for varied lengths of time to account for the different lengths of time they will need to succeed with the content at the stations.

4. Give directions one at a time to students who have difficulty with multistep tasks.

5. Model a task for English learners who need a bridge to understanding written directions for the task.

6. Increase or decrease the number of practice opportunities for a given skill based on readiness needs.

Additional Activities

Differentiating Products Based on Readiness

1. Ask some students to apply a concept or skill to a familiar context and more advanced students to apply the concept or skill to an unfamiliar context.

2. Provide resource materials in a student's first language, even though the product must be developed in English.

3. Provide a spell-check program for a student with a learning disability related to vocabulary and language.

4. Ask a student to turn in a draft a week before the final product is due because the student has undertaken a very complex product and needs not feel penalized for taking the risk.

5. Give some students who have difficulty with timelines a planner to map out when they will need to complete various components of a product in order to meet the submission deadline.

6. Provide models of effective student work at different levels of sophistication to match students' readiness levels.

Additional Activities

Differentiation and the Brain • © 2011 Solution Tree Press • solution-tree.com
Visit **go.solution-tree.com/instruction** to download this page.

CHAPTER 6

Differentiating in Response to Student Interest

The priority among most teachers seems to be to cover as much information as possible without regard to whether students are becoming interested in learning. . . . Despite our relatively heavy investment in education as a nation, we still do not seem to realize that teaching which does not consider the students' priorities is useless. It is wasteful to teach someone who is not interested and so is not motivated. . . . It is not enough for information to be clear and rational; it also has to be interesting. Learning has to be engaging and rewarding for students to learn.

—Mihaly Csikszentmihalyi, Kevin Rathunde, and Samuel Whalen, *Talented Teenagers: The Roots of Success and Failure*

At a time in our educational history when teaching seems equated with preparation for standardized tests, it would be easy to conclude that student interests have no place in the classroom, unless a student happens to be interested in some portion of the prescribed agenda. Research, our own personal experience, and classroom observation indicate, however, that student interests are anything but tangential to learning. They are conduits to motivation, relevance, and understanding. They even affect whether a struggling student will remain in school or become one of the increasing number of dropouts. A 2006 study asked nearly five hundred adolescents in twenty-five different cities, suburbs, and small towns why they left school (Bridgeland, DiIulio, & Morison, 2006). Although there are numerous reasons why students decide to drop out of school, 47 percent of the students surveyed said the main and most frequently cited reason they dropped out of school was that they did not find their classes interesting (see fig. 6.1, page 112). That is

47% Not interesting

one powerful message from students to educators that cannot be ignored. And yet, many teachers do largely ignore student interests, failing to link what students care about with the curriculum they feel responsible to teach.

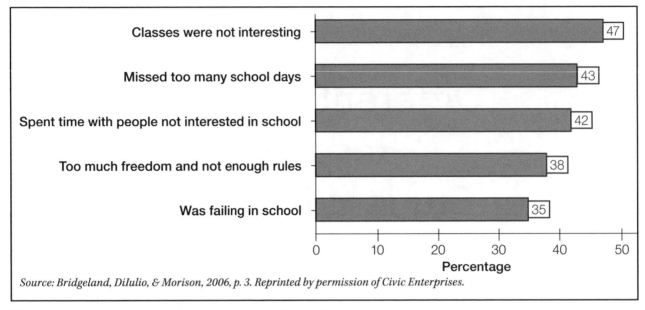

Source: Bridgeland, DiIulio, & Morison, 2006, p. 3. Reprinted by permission of Civic Enterprises.

Figure 6.1: Top five reasons for dropping out of school.

A Case in Point

Mr. Waymer felt pressure coming from all sides to raise student scores on the end-of-year standardized test. He had a sense of racing to a finish line that was coming at him and his students exponentially faster every day. He worked hard to make his lessons as efficient as possible. He aimed for, and generally achieved, a high level of time-on-task in his math class. He could not help but notice, however, that a number of his students, while cooperative, were lifeless in his class. Philip did what he had to do to make Cs in the class, because to do less was to incur endless lectures at home and the likelihood of being grounded. Suzanna paid attention but looked at her watch a lot. Andre sat in a slouch and frequently did not complete either class work or homework. One day, as Mr. Waymer tried to enlist his students' attention to a new topic, he said, "Okay, folks, listen up. This can be tricky, but it's really, really important for you to understand." From somewhere along the right side of the classroom came the comment, said softly and to no one in particular, "Yep. Gonna make us all better people."

Attending to Student Interest

Interest refers to a feeling or emotion that causes an individual to focus on or attend to something because it matters to that individual. Topics, events, or instances that are interesting to a person draw and hold that person's attention. They evoke curiosity or result in fascination. They occupy a person's thoughts, typically in a pleasant way, but they can cause concern. They result in a person's concentrating on the elements of interest and screening out other elements in a setting.

Attending to student interest in a classroom suggests a desire on the teacher's part to capitalize on those things a student cares about in order to facilitate learning. Attaching important content to student interests builds bridges between the student and critical knowledge, understanding, and skills. Therefore, effectively differentiating instruction in response to student interest rests on four key principles:

1. Interest recruits the brain's attention systems and stimulates cognitive involvement.

2. Any group of students at a given time is likely to have both common and varied interests.

3. When teachers know and address their students' interests in the context of curriculum and instruction, students are more likely to engage with the content.

4. Attention to student interests should focus students on essential knowledge, understanding, and skills, not divert students from them.

Differentiating instruction based on student interest does *not* suggest that a teacher should develop lessons that attend to all students' interests all of the time. It does *not* suggest that a student's interests are static. It does *not* suggest that all lessons should be interest focused. It does *not* suggest that essential content take a back seat to student interests. What interest-based differentiation *does* suggest is that when teachers know both their students and their content well, they have many opportunities to enhance teaching and learning by linking what matters most in a topic or discipline to what matters most to learners. Seen in that light, differentiation based on student interests has the potential to enhance learner efficacy and academic outcomes.

Why Addressing Student Interests Matters

A sizable body of theory and research indicates that interest-based study is generally linked to enhanced motivation to learn and to increased achievement in the long and short term (Hébert, 1993; Renninger, 1990, 1998; Tobias, 1994). For example, various theorists and researchers have proposed that interest-based study:

- Leads to greater student engagement, productivity, and achievement (Amabile, 1996; Torrance, 1995)

- Generates in learners a sense that learning is rewarding (Amabile, 1983; Bruner, 1961; Collins & Amabile, 1999; Sharan & Sharan, 1992)

- Contributes to a sense of competence, self-determination, and autonomy (Amabile, 1983; Bruner, 1961; Collins & Amabile, 1999; Sharan & Sharan, 1992)

- Encourages acceptance and persistence in the face of challenge (Csikszentmihalyi et al., 1993; Fulk & Montgomery-Grimes, 1994)

- Contributes to a positive, student-focused environment (National Research Council, 1999)

- Contributes to a culturally relevant classroom for students from non-majority backgrounds by allowing them to construct meaning, beginning with their own experiences (National Research Council, 1999)

- Promotes positive connections between student and teacher (Willingham, 2009)

Experts in this area also note that the use of choice, novelty, and prior knowledge in a particular academic context can help students who do not have strong personal interests engage with important content in that context (Hidi, 1990; Hidi & Anderson, 1992; Hidi & Berndorff, 1998). For instance, academic engagement and outcomes are enhanced when students are encouraged to pick reading material that is of interest to them (Carbonaro & Gamoran, 2002).

In addition, researchers note that when students find cognitive tasks interesting and satisfying at an early age, they are more likely to persist in seeking cognitive stimulation as they develop (Gottfried & Gottfried, 1996; Neitzel, Alexander, & Johnson, 2008). Similarly, young people who enter adolescence with strong interests are more likely to make the journey through adolescence successfully than those students who do not have strong personal interests (Csikszentmihalyi et al., 1993).

Further, learners who experience "flow"—or a sense of complete absorption such that time passes quickly when they are working in a particular area—are likely to develop successively more complex skills in that area because doing so promotes continued satisfaction (Csikszentmihalyi et al., 1993). Teachers are most effective in helping students find flow when they communicate high expectations with clear standards, support student efforts, are passionate about their content areas, and spend time planning to take advantage of students' interests and talents (Whalen, 1998). It is important to note the connection between readiness and interest. It is unlikely that work will remain interesting to a student if it is well beyond reach or already mastered. Thus, work that interests students will necessarily be at an appropriate challenge level for that student (Csikszentmihalyi et al., 1993; National Research Council, 1999).

> Students who find cognitive tasks interesting and satisfying at an early age are more likely to persist in seeking cognitive stimulation as they develop.

Neuroscience and Interest

Cognitive psychologists tend to describe interest in learning in terms of a set of behaviors that a person displays when involved in an activity. These behaviors include increased attention, greater concentration, pleasant feelings of applied effort, increased willingness to learn, and engaging in the learning activity freely, with persistence, energy, and intensity. Psychologists also describe two types of interest:

1. *Individual interest* refers to the ongoing preference that an individual has for a particular subject or activity. This interest develops slowly over time and leads to increased knowledge and skills, appreciation, and positive feelings. Examples would be a person's love of playing a musical instrument or delving into astronomy.

2. *Situational interest* is provoked by certain conditions in the environment that elicit positive feelings, although it may include some negative emotions as well. It is a more immediate reaction that may or may not endure. An example would be visiting a planetarium to discover how it replicates the night sky indoors.

Both types of interest include a positive affective component, tend to be specifically related to content, and result from the interaction of the individual with the environment. It is possible that situational and individual interests themselves interact. For example, individual interest in a subject may help a student get past a boring presentation. Situational interest generated by a topic because of the novel way it was presented may sustain motivation, even when the student has no particular interest in the topic. In addition, situational interest may develop over time into individual interest. For instance, reading teachers may use the situational interest that a student has for a particular story to develop long-term individual interest in reading.

The question arises whether interest is a separate mental entity or the result of a collection of behaviors that occur when an individual is intrinsically motivated to learn more about a topic or skill. Neuroscientific studies at this time have not isolated any neural networks that could be related specifically to a singular entity that defines "interest." Nonetheless, many of the behaviors that researchers use to describe interest—especially motivation—have found considerable support from studies in cognitive neuroscience. Findings from these studies show that high motivation leads to greater attention and increased willingness to learn (Engelmann & Pessoa, 2007; Goldberg, 2001; Raymond, 2009) and to persistence (Vansteenkiste, Simons, Lens, Sheldon, & Deci, 2004; Vollmeyer & Rheinberg, 2000). High motivation leads to greater interest, and high interest is intrinsically motivating.

A surprising finding about motivation came from an imaging study that concentrated on motivation to learn versus motivation to gain a monetary payment (Mizuno et al., 2008). The results showed that motivation to learn

Many of the behaviors that researchers use to describe interest—especially motivation—have found support from studies in cognitive neuroscience.

activated an area of the brain called the *putamen* (see fig. 6.2), and that the higher the motivation, the greater the change in the signals within the putamen. Monetary motivation also activated the putamen, but the intensity was not related to the size of the monetary payment. The researchers concluded that (1) the putamen is critical for motivation in different domains and (2) the extent of activity of the putamen may be crucial to the motivation that drives academic achievement and thus academic success. One might also infer that the motivation a student experiences when learning something interesting is more rewarding than a potential financial gain.

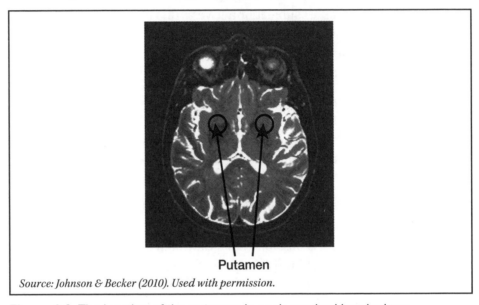

Source: Johnson & Becker (2010). Used with permission.

Figure 6.2: The location of the putamen in each cerebral hemisphere.

Seven Themes for Addressing Student Interest in the Classroom

The reasons that it is beneficial to attend to student interest are multifaceted and interconnected. At the very least, connecting important content with student interests improves the learning environment, supports student attention and engagement, provides a foundation for working with complex ideas and developing complex skills, supports persistence in the face of challenge, creates a sense of accomplishment and satisfaction in work, and builds a sense of student agency or independence. In the end, these factors, singly and in combination, can significantly enhance student learning.

We have identified seven themes that can help teachers think about and plan for student interests in the classroom. Each theme can draw on and contribute to student interest—that is, to sense-making, engagement, persistence, and ownership. And each one has a place in planning for curriculum and instruction that are responsive to student needs and differences.

1. "Hey, I've heard of that before!" Starting with illustrations and applications that are familiar to students is often more interesting to

them and can help them move from more concrete to more abstract, and from simpler to more complex, understandings and skills.

2. "That sounds like my house!" It is useful for all students to see themselves in what they learn about. That experience is more common, however, for students in the classroom's majority culture. Administrators and teachers tend to rely on the settings in which they grew up—and in which they were educated in the majority culture—to provide books, heroes, celebrations, ways of working, and illustrations that depict cultural or economic contexts. Ensuring cultural relevance, fit, or familiarity for every student in a classroom casts a wider net of interest and success.

3. "This stuff is cool!" When teachers know their content deeply, they can easily craft curriculum as a lively narrative that is rich with meaning, surprises, intrigue, and stories rather than as a series of data bits and isolated skills. When curriculum is designed to be interesting, it is more memorable for more students, not less so.

4. "Man, he's an interesting teacher!" When teachers respond both to content requirements and to student interests by systematically varying the way they teach and the ways in which students can show what they know, the class is much livelier and much more interesting to more students. More students succeed and, not surprisingly, more students find learning interesting.

5. "You know, she's really an interesting person!" When a teacher shares her own interests—beyond those of the content she teaches—with her students, they benefit from a good model of a person with a multifaceted life, and they can come to understand more fully how learning enriches life in all its aspects. If the teacher then helps students see how she uses those interests to connect with and illuminate the content they share, there is a dual benefit.

6. "I see myself in this subject." Not every kid is interested in math or in history or in art or in any other school subject. However, every kid does bring interests to class. Further, in the real world, content is interrelated, not segmented in the way we divide it in school. Mathematics is highly relevant to sports, to music, and to politics. History is a mirror of the street corner. Poetry is lyrics waiting for a musical score, and it pokes at everybody's life. Teachers who grasp the power of student interest find critical moments to say, "Here's the important skill we're practicing today, but you have a choice of whether to use that skill to address a problem in our school, a dilemma in our country, or a scenario from the future." Or they say, "Everyone needs to read a biography to help us understand the characteristics of good biography. I've brought in biographies of athletes, actors, scientists, villains, heroes, leaders, and inventors from many countries and time periods. I hope

you'll find a book that links up with things you care about. However, I'm also open to your suggesting other biographies."

7. "Isn't there some way I can learn about . . . ?" Sometimes students bring well-developed interests to school with them that are not reflected in the curriculum. In some cases, they have a deep hunger to learn more about that topic, and school may be the only place or the best place to do so. A teacher who wants to extend the curiosity and learning processes of such students finds ways to make space, give permission, and provide guidance for such learning. At other times, students bring (or develop in class) simpler questions that itch for an answer. These, too, provide opportunities for teachers to make room for student interests in the classroom and to erase some of the artificial segmentation of knowledge that often characterizes school. In both instances, strategies such as anchor activities (tasks to which students turn when they complete required work), inquiry centers, enrichment centers, and independent studies allow students to investigate areas or questions of personal interest.

The Role of Classroom Elements in Planning for Interest-Based Differentiation

As is the case with readiness differentiation, differentiating in response to student interest has implications for the five key classroom elements: learning environment, curriculum, assessment, management, and instruction. Understanding those implications as well as how the elements interact to support effective interest-based differentiation enables a teacher to plan more effectively and to carry out those plans more efficiently.

Learning Environment

As we have emphasized, learning is supported by an environment that feels safe, affirming, challenging, and supportive to each student in that environment. Teacher belief in each student's worth and potential is a catalyst for teacher-student connections and ultimately for building a community of learners that functions something like a team—with each member drawing on the strengths of the others and contributing to their development and success. Certainly these important environmental attributes are enhanced when a teacher seeks to understand student interests and to incorporate those interests into curriculum and instruction in substantive ways. In such an environment, students are likely to believe that they matter to the teacher, that their interests and experiences have value, that both their common and unique interests contribute to learning, and that their varied backgrounds extend the shared perspectives of the class. Further, an environment that is rich in learning materials and opportunities—another likely attribute of a classroom that addresses student interests as one facet of differentiation—supports academic, emotional, and social growth.

Curriculum

While curriculum is shaped in significant measure by prescribed standards, a set of standards is *not* a curriculum any more than a sack of groceries is a dinner. How educators conceive, organize, and share required content knowledge is the art of curriculum design. Clearly, the core goal of curriculum is to ensure that students master essential knowledge, understanding, and skills so that they can not only retain but also apply and transfer what they learn. Nonetheless, there is not only ample room for student interests in that goal, but designing curriculum with student interests in mind can contribute to the goal in important ways. The truth of an essential understanding can be written in many ways. Crafting the understandings in language that relates to the experiences of students is wise. Further, analogies often activate information in long-term memory, thereby helping students grasp unfamiliar and complex ideas. Drawing analogies from multiple areas of student interest simply enhances their power to illuminate—whether the teacher generates them or calls on students to do so.

> A set of standards is not a curriculum any more than a sack of groceries is a dinner.

All good curriculum provides opportunities for students to try out, make sense of, or come to "own" the knowledge, understanding, and skills specified as essential. Learning will most likely be enhanced if, at least some of the time, students can try out what they need to learn in areas of interest to them. Finally, good curriculum weaves a narrative—a coherent story that helps students understand concepts such as cause and effect, sequence, main idea and illustration, and so on. Sometimes the story derives the greatest meaning by paralleling and drawing from the students' own stories or the stories of people, places, events, and times that capture their attention. Levy (1996) talks about the importance of steering the currents of student enthusiasm to the shores of the required curriculum. That is the balance that quality curriculum achieves. Student interests in such curriculum contribute to, rather than detract from, what is essential.

Assessment

Student interests intersect with assessment in at least three ways:

1. Preassessment is an important vehicle for beginning to understand what interests students bring to school with them. Simple surveys give students a chance to share what they like to do in their spare time, what subjects they have found most interesting in school, or things they would like to learn about as the year goes on.

2. Similarly, formative assessment—both formal and informal—can continue to inform the teacher's understanding of what is interesting to students, both in general and in particular segments of study.

3. Both formative and summative assessments can be developed with student interests in mind. As long as the unit's essential knowledge, understanding, and skills remain the clear focus of the assessment, the applications of those elements to various interest areas is not only legitimate but often advantageous in promoting student engagement with the assessment and encouraging transfer of ideas and skills to varied contexts.

Classroom Management

Just as we saw with readiness-differentiated classrooms, flexibility is a hallmark of classrooms that are differentiated based on students' interests. Teacher and student comfort with the flexible use of time, space, materials, student groups, and tasks makes it possible for students to draw on, pursue, and share different interests when appropriate. This sort of flexibility also enables the teacher to work with individuals and small groups of students on interest-focused tasks and applications, providing coaching on skills of inquiry—such as planning, use of resources, evaluation of progress, collaboration, and revision—as well as required content. Most of the remainder of this chapter focuses on the role of instruction—the fifth classroom element—in effectively addressing the diverse student interests that inevitably exist in a given classroom.

Some Guidelines for Differentiating in Response to Student Interest

It should not be a surprise that some of the guidelines for planning and teaching with student interests in mind are similar to those offered in chapter 5 for addressing variations in student readiness. The following guidelines make clear once again that effective teaching stems from relatively constant principles and practices.

- Identify and articulate in student language what students should know, understand, and be able to do as a result of the unit of study you will be differentiating. Conveying this information ensures that you and your students are clear about the destination everyone is expected to reach. Including student interests in teaching and learning plans ensures that more students arrive at the destination more readily.

- Consider using a preassessment of student interests. This can be in the form of a checklist or a questionnaire. Young students or students who struggle with reading or writing find it helpful if they can respond to icons or images rather than words, if they can audio-record answers, or if they can give answers verbally and have someone else write them down. The preassessment can take place early in the school year or at the outset of a new unit of study. It can focus on the students' personal interests or ask them which of the required topics are most interesting to them, or both. Figure 6.3 (page 122) provides a sample interest survey.

- As a way of connecting with your students, find small time segments to share your interests with them, individually and as a class, modeling the pleasure a good learner derives from learning about many aspects of life.

- Be purposeful in providing opportunities for students to talk about or otherwise share their interests (both general and content-specific) as the year goes on. Develop and use a system for recording what you learn about student interests so that you can retain and refer to this information as you plan lessons and student groupings. For example, one teacher used index cards to record student interests over time (see fig. 6.4, page 123). She flipped through the cards quickly to refresh her memory as she planned presentations, activities, and products. She could also sort the cards easily to form like-interest groups or groups of students with varied interests, depending on the nature and requirements of a task.

- When you plan curriculum, draw on your knowledge of student interests to (1) state essential understandings in ways that are relevant to student backgrounds, experiences, and interests; (2) build in activities that draw on student interests; (3) use a variety of student groupings based on both similar and dissimilar interests; (4) incorporate anchor activities and extension activities that encourage exploration of student interests; (5) include instructional strategies that invite attention to students' varied interests; (6) develop assessments that incorporate student interests as a means of engaging students with important ideas and skills; and (7) make useful connections with other content areas.

- Based on preassessment information and other knowledge about your students as a class, think about ways in which you can include examples, analogies, stories, and applications in your instruction that you know will interest many students.

- Based on preassessment information and other knowledge about your students as individuals, refine plans for activities, products, extensions, and groupings to focus on the specific interests of individual students.

- Remember the connection between readiness and interest. While students may be able to work at a somewhat more complex level in areas of high interest, it is still true that they will not grow when tasks are well above or below their current level of functioning. Further,

To Teach You Better . . .

I want to do the best job I can in helping you succeed as a student and as a human being. The better I know you, the better job I can do. I hope you will answer the questions below honestly. I will use the information as I plan our time together.

1. What do you most enjoy learning about or doing in your spare time?

2. Describe a time when you were working on something or learning about something and it felt like time flew by.

3. Which topics in school (any class) have you found the most satisfying? Explain why.

4. What topics or areas in history have you found most interesting or do you think might be interesting this year?

5. What do you think makes a class interesting?

Figure 6.3: An interest survey for students.

tasks that initially seem interesting are likely to become frustrating or boring if they are outside a student's current challenge zone. Thus, materials, directions, models, and expectations need to be just above a student's current level of functioning. Moreover, supports or scaffolding remain necessary to help students succeed at the new level of challenge.

- Be sure that plans for the flexible grouping of students include interest-based groups. Some of these groups should be designed to help students with similar interests connect key content with those interests. Others should be designed to bring together students with disparate interests. In this mix, the students gain insight into important issues, develop broader perspectives on issues, or understand how essential understandings and skills apply in a variety of settings.

```
┌─────────────────────────────────────────┐
│        Student Name: Cassie Landry        │
│                                           │
│                                           │
│                                           │
│                                           │
│                                           │
│                                           │
│                                           │
│                                           │
│ Period: 4                                 │
└─────────────────────────────────────────┘
```

Music	Hobbies	People	Other
Sports	Books	Events	

Figure 6.4: The front and back of an index card for recording student interests.

- Provide various opportunities and formats for students to share how they have connected essential content with their interests. When such sharing is structured appropriately, students should reinforce and extend essential ideas and skills, see themselves and others as contributing members of the learning community, and develop a growing appreciation for their own interests as well as the interests of others. Ensure that directions, rubrics, and models that support student work keep students focused on the lesson's or unit's essential knowledge, understanding, and skills within the context of the students' areas of interest. Interest-based tasks should align tightly with the unit's or lesson's KUDs.

- Think about classroom procedures and routines that need to be in place for the interest-based options to work as they should. Then, make sure that students are ready to participate successfully in those routines. (See chapter 8.)

- As students work independently on interest-based tasks and applications, use your time to meet with individuals and small groups of students, monitoring progress, coaching for success, and noting what you learn so that your understanding of student strengths and needs grows consistently.

- Continue to study your students and elicit their input on interest-based approaches that they find helpful in mastering essential content and on ways they would fine-tune current approaches. Ask them to suggest additional interest-based ideas.

- Seek input from students on how they are feeling about their proficiency with essential knowledge, understanding, and skills.

- Keep studying your content to understand more and more fully what makes it interesting and dynamic and how it relates to a variety of human endeavors, so that you become more comfortable with and skillful at connecting the content with student interests.

Exercise 6.1 (page 131) offers a checklist for reflecting on teacher practice in addressing student interests.

Differentiating Content, Process, and Product Based on Student Interest

As with readiness differentiation, it is useful to think about how teachers can differentiate content, process, and product based on interest. Thinking systematically about opportunities to link each of the elements with student interests provides a wider range of teaching and learning opportunities.

Content

You will recall that differentiating content can entail either differentiating the stuff students need to master (the KUDs) or differentiating how students gain access to it. You will probably also recall that the goal in differentiation is most often to vary how students access key content rather than to vary the content itself. That is certainly true in terms of essential understandings. In terms of interest-based differentiation, the essential knowledge, understanding, and skills will generally remain constant for students. In other words, the same KUDs will be central to each interest-based option. The reason, of course, is that interest-based differentiation is one way to maximize the likelihood that each student will succeed with key content. Therefore, the interest-based options are in service of the KUDs.

True, a student who reads about pioneers in medicine will come away with some different information from her classmates who read about pioneers beneath the ocean or those who read about pioneers for human rights. However, if the task is structured appropriately, all the students will, for example, focus on the *essential* concepts and principles related to the nature of pioneers. What, for example, makes a pioneer different from a traveler or a discoverer? Further, students who pursue extension options or independent inquiries will also come away with content that is different from what their peers have studied. Here, too, however, that content expands rather than supplants the KUDs.

To differentiate content based on student interests, a teacher might do the following:

- Provide books, articles, websites, videos, podcasts, expert presentations, and other resources that can help students relate essential content (KUDs) to their areas of interest.

- Use illustrations of complex ideas that relate to student interests to help students move from familiar and satisfying contexts to less familiar and more taxing contexts.

- Show examples of skills applications in areas of student interest to help students see how the skills are applied in varied and real-world settings.

- Use examples, analogies, and applications that mirror the cultures, languages, and experiences of all students in the class.

- Spotlight high-interest examples from the discipline that represent key ideas effectively.

- Share ways in which personal interests intersect with essential knowledge, understanding, and skills in a unit or lesson.

Process

Recall that process begins when students move from taking in content from outside sources (including teachers, text, and the media) to actively making sense of and trying out or applying it themselves. We often refer to process as "activities" or "sense-making." Process provides students with time to practice what they need to master and can occur both in class and at home. To differentiate process based on student interests, a teacher might do the following:

- Provide opportunities for students to apply skills in relevant areas of interest.

- Provide opportunities for students to establish, test, or expand essential understandings in areas of interest—including areas of high cultural relevance.

- Provide models of student (or expert) work in relevant areas of interest.

- Structure opportunities for students to share examples of ways in which essential skills and/or understandings are revealed or apply in areas of like or dissimilar interests.

Product

Recall that products are a kind of summative assessment. They occur at the end of major segments of learning (although students may begin working on them earlier in a unit) and should be designed to enable students to effectively demonstrate what they know, understand, and can do as a result of that segment of study. Tests are a kind of product but are usually limited to measuring knowledge and skills—often outside of a meaningful context. Products that are more authentic in nature and call on students to apply and transfer what they have learned typically integrate knowledge, understanding, and skills. To differentiate products based on student interest, a teacher might do the following:

- Develop authentic product assignments in which the KUDs that are assessed remain the same, but students can use them to address issues or propose solutions to problems in different areas or topics of interest—including interest areas that students propose.

- Develop tests in which applications are drawn from areas likely to be of interest to many students.

- Encourage and scaffold independent studies or inquiries in which students apply and extend key content in areas of personal interest.

- Encourage and facilitate student work with experts or mentors in an area of shared interest to apply and extend key content.

- Ask students to set personal goals for their interest-focused products based on their particular interests.

Exercise 6.2 (page 134) offers some additional examples of ways in which teachers might differentiate content, process, and product in response to student interests.

Differentiating With Expert Groups and Sidebar Studies

This chapter contains numerous strategies for addressing student interests. We will take a closer look here at two commonly used strategies: expert groups and sidebar studies.

Expert Groups

Expert groups enable students with common interests to learn more deeply about a particular aspect of a unit of study and then to help the teacher teach the class about it. This strategy enables students to engage more complex cognitive processes that will build extensive and long-lasting neural networks. The following process generally works well in establishing expert groups and supporting their success:

- The teacher determines some topics in a unit of study that address student interests and seem to lend themselves well to student investigation and sharing with the rest of the class. Typically, two or three possible topics will be adequate for a unit. In some instances, only one aspect of the unit will seem appropriate for an expert-group investigation.

- The teacher offers students an opportunity to join an expert group—generally with some limitations on the number of students in a group and the number of groups that will be working during a given unit. If students do not have a particular interest in the topics the teacher suggests, they might suggest alternatives for the teacher's approval. It is also fine if there is no expert group for one or several units. When introducing possible topics, the teacher should frame the investigation in ways that tap into student curiosity and shape the parameters of the group's work.

- If an expert group surfaces, the teacher meets with the group early in the unit to provide guidelines for working, timetables for planning work, a rubric for quality work, and models of high-quality work from other expert groups. Students in the group make a plan for their work with the teacher, including check-in dates as key components of their work are completed. It is particularly important at the outset of their work that the students and teacher be clear on the knowledge, understanding, and skills that must be represented in their presentation to the class.

- The teacher checks with students in the group informally several times a week and provides formal feedback at the designated check-in times.

- Several days before the expert group participates in teaching a lesson, the group members meet with the teacher to develop the lesson plan that they will use. The plan must include a way for the class to work with the important ideas or skills in the lesson and a way for the group members to assess student understanding as the lesson ends. Students play a key role in developing the lesson plan; the teacher plays the role of coach and facilitator.

- The expert group and the teacher teach the lesson at the appropriate point in the unit, ensuring active participation by class members. The group members also conduct and review the formative assessment and debrief with the teacher about the lesson as a whole.

The process is less complex than it may seem. Most of the meetings with the teacher take place during class, while other students are working with assigned tasks. Students in the expert group are given released time from some class activities and from some homework to allow them to learn about their topic and plan to share their findings. Once one or two expert groups have co-taught with the teacher, the system becomes familiar to the class, and everyone plays a role in shaping the process as the year moves forward.

Often, students will volunteer for expert groups around topics that have been their longtime interests and about which they already have a good bit of knowledge. Sometimes, however, students volunteer for an expert group because they want to learn more about a topic that seems intriguing to them but about which they know little or nothing. In either case, as long as there is a good balance between teacher-provided structure and student autonomy, expert groups affirm and extend student interests and independence.

Our first "In the Classroom" scenario is an example of using expert groups in an elementary-level social studies lesson.

In the Classroom
Social Studies Lesson, Expert Group (Elementary School)

Students in Mrs. Regan's class were about to begin a study of the American Revolution. One part of the unit would focus on the war's costs and benefits to young people. An essential question for the unit was "What is revolutionary in a revolution and for whom?" As the unit began, Mrs. Regan asked students to share what they knew about how the Revolutionary War affected their town. Some students had a good bit of information to offer, but many did not. She then explained to the students that the war had been revolutionary for people of their age and asked them how they thought those young lives might have been revolutionized. After some discussion, she proposed an expert group that could help the class answer the question "What was revolutionary about the Revolutionary War for young people in our town?" Four students volunteered to be in the expert group, and Mrs. Regan met with them the following day to share an expert group packet she had developed over the past several years. The packet included the information and materials they would need to begin their investigation and planning.

To come up with answers to the question the teacher assigned them, the students ultimately used books from the school and the local library, conversations with a local historian, a couple of websites suggested by the historian, a search of an old graveyard in their area, and courthouse documents. When they presented their lesson, they asked their classmates to take on the roles of young people they had found out about in their search and to propose their own answers to the key question as the class period progressed.

As a result of their work, the students in the expert group gained a much deeper and more personal sense of history. Their classmates also saw a side of the time period they would not have encountered otherwise. Both groups made many connections to the lesson through the remainder of the unit and as they studied other time periods later in the year. One student said, "I guess I never thought about history happening to kids before."

Sidebar Studies

A sidebar study is an investigation students conduct as a unit of study progresses in their classroom. It is called a sidebar study because it takes place outside of class time and does not interrupt the flow of the curriculum. A sidebar study also allows students to explore an interest "on the side" that integrates directly with the required curriculum. The studies are usually conducted by individual students, but small groups could complete them as well. A sidebar study generally lasts at least two or three weeks to give students time to pursue the investigation as well as to complete required class work and homework—although teachers often assign less homework during a sidebar study. When a sidebar study is successful, students will gain important information and insights from their investigation as a unit unfolds, with the result that they will participate in the unit far more, and far more enthusiastically, because it becomes increasingly relevant to them.

As is the case with expert groups, it is important for teachers to give students specific guidelines for planning and conducting their investigations as well as the questions to be answered by the investigations. Students should also understand from the outset what their options are for reporting their findings and what quality would look like in both their working processes and final products.

Our second "In the Classroom" scenario is an example of using a sidebar study in a middle school mathematics class.

> A sidebar study allows students to explore a curriculum-related topic of interest outside of class.

In the Classroom
Mathematics Lesson, Sidebar Study (Middle School)

Mr. Mercado worked hard to help his students see mathematics as a living language that helped people in their everyday lives and that made a difference in the world. Early in the year, he asked his pre-algebra students if they knew whose lives would be diminished in some significant way if mathematics did not exist. Not surprisingly, the students initially found it humorous that people's lives could be "messed up" without mathematics. One student exclaimed, "Man, my life is messed up *because* math exists!"

Mr. Mercado asked his students to find adults whose hobby or work seemed interesting and who were willing to make the case that mathematics was essential to their work or hobby. The person chosen could be an adult at school, a parent or other relative, a neighbor, someone at church, someone who worked with them in an extracurricular activity, or someone famous. Whoever they selected had to be approved by the teacher and had to agree to communicate with them at least twice to explain and demonstrate specifically how the absence of mathematics would negatively affect their lives. Students could write up their interviews, using sketches and diagrams as necessary; create a brief PowerPoint synopsis of their interviews, using a variety of visuals to answer the question; or contribute to a podcast on the question, emceed by the teacher. Presentations could not be more than three minutes long. The students had to introduce the interviewee, briefly explain the person's job or hobby, use the person's own words to make a case for the necessity of mathematics in his or her life, and provide one concrete example of how mathematics made the person's life better.

Students found it surprisingly easy to recruit interviewees. Their subjects included athletes, physicians, musicians, engineers, businesspeople, the school principal, architects, scout leaders, collectors of various items, and a grandfather trying to make the most of his retirement funds. Mr. Mercado noted that students began volunteering examples from their interviews within a day or two from the time the sidebar assignment was given. The student contributions continued throughout the year, whenever what the students were studying intersected with the lives of the people they had interviewed. Mr. Mercado often used pieces of the PowerPoints, paragraphs from the essays, and snippets of the podcasts to remind students that what they were learning at a given time had, as he said, "a fan club out there in the streets."

A Better Scenario

Mr. Waymer tells his students that they may, from time to time, think they've stumbled into the wrong room because they will find themselves in a crime lab, a courtroom, Las Vegas, or someplace else they didn't anticipate. He uses clips from popular TV shows, segments from the news, and excerpts from novels to introduce math concepts, to create problems for students to solve, and to demonstrate key math skills at work in the world.

He surveys his students about their interests two or three times a year and also engages them in conversations about what they enjoy doing. He uses what he learns to create word problems in which the students are characters and their interests play a role. When it is appropriate for content requirements, he provides options for assessments so that the students can select areas of interest in which to apply key skills.

Mr. Waymer is finding his teaching more satisfying since he has started looking for ways to make math livelier for his students. Not only are students more energetic and engaged, but they have become his allies in looking for math around them in the world. They now bring him some of his best examples, which he in turn shares with his classes.

Exercise 6.1

A Checklist for Differentiating Instruction Based on Student Interest

Reflect on your curriculum for a unit, semester, or year, and then respond to the following questions. After you finish, review your responses and think about whether you should consider making any changes to your instruction in order to respond more effectively to students' varied interests. Building administrators can use this activity at a faculty meeting to discuss the school's progress in working toward differentiating instruction in response to student interests. The questions could also provide a framework for planning professional development and for helping teachers incorporate differentiation based on student interest into their instructional plans.

1. Do you clearly articulate KUDs for units and for lessons?

2. Do you ensure that students are clear about KUDs as they do interest-based tasks so that each task focuses on what is essential about the lesson or unit?

3. Have you thought about potential high-interest areas in your subject or unit?

4. Have you built interest-based options into your curriculum?

5. Have you developed a narrative for your subject or unit—a "story" that will help students make sense of the content and find it memorable?

6. Are you aware of the various cultural backgrounds of students in your class(es)? Do you understand them well enough to have a sense of what is relevant and interesting to them?

7. Do you look for and use examples of your content's being used by a variety of individuals in a variety of contexts that are likely to be of interest to students?

8. Have you developed and administered a student-interest survey?

9. Do you listen to student conversations and engage students in conversations about their interests?

page 1 of 3

10. Do you have a systematic way of recording what you hear so that you can develop and draw on an increasing sense of what captures students' interest?

11. Do you use what you learn about student interests to inform your instructional planning?

12. Do you consider critical readiness needs in planning interest-based assignments?

13. Do you use examples from students' lives and interests to help them move from familiar to more complex applications and understandings?

14. Do you use student interests to help correct student deficit areas and/or to enhance student proficiency areas?

15. Do you make time to share your interests with students?

16. Have you looked for ways to use contemporary technologies as teaching and learning tools?

17. Do you plan for both similar and dissimilar interest-based groups as part of each unit?

18. Do you use strategies such as sidebar studies, expert groups, learning centers, jigsaw independent studies, anchor activities, and other approaches that invite attention to student interests?

19. Do you provide interest-based work options to students, as appropriate, and do you invite them to propose interest-based options as well?

20. Do you provide clear guidelines for work and quality when students are doing interest-based assignments, so that they are prepared to succeed?

21. Have you developed classroom routines and procedures that support students in working with varied tasks and in varied group configurations?

22. Have you prepared students to work effectively with, and contribute to the refinement of, those routines?

23. Do you use student work time to meet with individuals and small groups about interests and interest-based assignments?

Differentiation and the Brain • © 2011 Solution Tree Press • solution-tree.com

Visit **go.solution-tree.com/instruction** to download this page.

Exercise 6.2

Activities for Differentiating Content, Process, and Product Based on Student Interest

Here are some suggestions for activities that can help you differentiate content, process, and product based on your students' interests. Add to each section other activities that you and your colleagues feel are appropriate. Building administrators can use this activity at a faculty meeting to discuss the school's progress in working toward differentiating these three components based on student interest.

Differentiating Content Based on Interest

1. Use expert presentations that demonstrate essential knowledge, understanding, and skills in contexts of interest to students.

2. Use mini-lessons with small groups to connect key content with students' areas of interest.

3. Offer books on a variety of topics and in a variety of genres that relate to essential content.

4. Use contemporary media as resources for teaching.

5. Provide free reading material on a wide range of topics.

6. Ensure that topical resources reflect a variety of cultures and backgrounds.

7. Develop (and invite students to develop) anchor activities that reflect a wide range of student interests related to key content.

   Additional Activities

Differentiating Process Based on Interest

1. Use interest centers designed around topics within a unit that are of special interest to students.

2. Facilitate short- or long-term mentorships in which students will extend and apply key content knowledge in contexts of interest to them.

3. Use expert groups or jigsaw groups that allow students to specialize in facets of a required topic that are of particular interest to them.

4. Use simulations that are relevant to the essential content and allow students to play roles and address problems or issues that are of particular interest to them.

5. Use contemporary resources to support student exploration, application, testing, and extension of essential content.

Additional Activities

Differentiating Product Based on Interest

1. Offer "Let's Make a Deal" product options through which students can propose products that use KUDs in relevant areas of personal interest.

2. Invite (or ask students to invite) experts in students' areas of interest to help develop product criteria and/or to provide feedback on student products in interest-based areas.

3. Enable students to use contemporary media as tools to demonstrate knowledge, understanding, and skills.

4. Differentiate test items to ensure high cultural relevance while holding KUDs constant.

Additional Activities

CHAPTER

Differentiating in Response to Student Learning Profile

If she only knew . . . that I like to make stuff during science class, she would let us make rockets like Mrs. Bagen's class. Instead, we read about rockets from a book. . . . If she only knew . . . that I need to talk if I'm going to learn, she wouldn't send me to the principal's office so much. She says my talking is disruptive in the classroom. She's the only person talking. In my opinion, that's disruptive.

—Jeff Gray and Heather Thomas, *If She Only Knew Me*

Most people can learn most things in more than one way. However, while one approach may make the process of learning seem more natural or accessible to a particular learner, another approach may confound the process. Although individual preferences for learning are probably somewhat fluid, depending on the circumstances or context, a mismatch between how a student learns best in a particular context and how the teacher expects the student to learn can greatly impede the learning process.

The Elements of Learning Profile

Learning profile is an umbrella term that encompasses four aspects of how individuals learn, how they process what they need to learn, or how they think about, remember, and prefer to use what they learn (Tomlinson, 1999, 2001). In other words, learning profile relates to how people "come at" learning. Research has established that the four overlapping areas encompassed by learning profile are learning styles, intelligence preferences, culture, and gender (Tomlinson et al., 2003).

A Case in Point

Jake likes his history class. He thinks Ms. Powell's lectures are clear, and if he writes down the information from the lectures, he can memorize it and generally make As and Bs on her tests. Some of his friends, however, don't share his opinion. Samet has difficulty with the torrent of words pouring from the teacher's mouth every day. He can't write the words fast enough, so he draws sketches trying to capture what he understands from the lectures. He gets poor grades on his history notebook because Ms. Powell can't understand his sketches. He also does poorly on tests because, although he grasps key ideas and events, his responses are weak on details. Elsbeth finds the lectures boring but takes good notes. Even so, she struggles when major papers are due. Students must give Ms. Powell a detailed outline of the papers a week before they are due. Somehow, Elsbeth understands the structure of her papers only after she completes them. She stays up late for a number of nights before outlines are due so that she can complete the paper and generate her outline. Bondi says he just dislikes studying about a bunch of dead people. He doesn't see what history has to do with the world he lives in—especially since all the dead people Ms. Powell talks about came from a different part of the world than he did.

Learning Styles

Learning style theory and models stem from the belief that people learn differently and will learn more effectively when the circumstances of learning match their particular approaches to learning. Learning style is often perceived as more acquired and adaptable than inborn and fixed. Further, learning style theory suggests that while some individuals may have very strong preferences for some approaches to learning, virtually all people can and do learn in more than one way. The idea is to help individuals find those approaches that work best for them and to use those approaches to facilitate their success.

A number of theorists and educators have proposed learning style models, including David Kolb (1984) and Bernice McCarthy (1987). Perhaps the best known among them are Kenneth and Rita Dunn (1993), who have worked with learning styles since the 1970s. Their model is organized around five categories: environmental, emotional, sociological, physiological, and psychological preferences or learning styles. The following learning preferences stem from these categories:

- Lighter versus darker environments
- Silence versus noise when working
- Cooler versus warmer rooms
- Sitting up straight versus reclining while learning
- Intrinsic motivation to complete a task versus motivation through adult prompting
- Completing one task at a time versus multitasking

- Independence as a learner versus dependence on adult prompting/ coaching

- Highly structured tasks versus open-ended tasks

- Working alone versus working with one peer versus working as part of a team

- Predictable routines versus variation

- Listening versus watching versus touching to learn

- Working at one time of day versus another

- Whole-to-part versus part-to-whole approaches

- Moving versus remaining still while learning

Add to these possible learning preferences others that emerge from the work of different psychologists or educators, and a significant challenge for teachers becomes how to understand, let alone address, so many categories. We will discuss this issue later in the chapter.

Intelligence Preferences

Intelligences or intelligence preferences also relate to individual learning preferences. While learning styles are often viewed as more acquired and flexible, intelligence preference models present intelligences as more fixed and inborn. Nonetheless, experts in intelligence preference models also note that virtually all individuals work in all intelligence areas. Not doing so would result in some degree of disability because people need to draw on all of the areas to function effectively. The idea with intelligence preference theories is to determine an individual's area(s) of strength and to use approaches to teaching and learning that allow and encourage the student to work and grow in those areas. In addition, however, multiple intelligence theorists advocate giving learners guided opportunities to develop intelligences other than those in which they are strongest.

The two key intelligence preference models were developed by Howard Gardner (1983/2004; 2006) and Robert Sternberg (1985). Gardner uses a multifaceted process to determine that an intelligence area exists, and he designates an intelligence area only when a number of criteria are met. He has proposed eight intelligence areas, noting a ninth area as a possibility. One of Gardner's goals is to help educators understand both the presence and the value of all his proposed intelligences in students. He notes that schools often stress a relatively narrow swath of verbal and mathematical intelligences, to the near exclusion of the others, and he is an advocate for classrooms where multiple intelligences can flourish. Table 7.1 (page 140) lists and briefly describes Gardner's proposed intelligence preferences.

Table 7.1: Howard Gardner's Designated and Possible Intelligences

Intelligence	Description
Verbal-Linguistic	Sensitivity to and/or appreciation of words and language; ability to use words effectively for self-expression and communication and to remember information; ability to learn languages
Logical-Mathematical	Ability with numbers, logic, deduction, and the processes of scientific inquiry; ability with procedural and systematic thinking
Visual-Spatial	Ability to see objects in space; ability to recognize, create, and/or appreciate patterns in space; appreciation of color, shape, and form
Musical-Rhythmic	Ability to compose, perform, and/or appreciate sound, tone, and musical sequences; sensitivity to sounds
Bodily-Kinesthetic	Ability to use the body to address or solve problems; ability to use the body for self-expression and communication; ability to coordinate body and mind effectively
Interpersonal	Ability to understand, communicate with, and effectively work with others; ability to appreciate the motivations and goals of others and to work with them toward achieving those goals; ability to lead
Intrapersonal	Ability to understand one's own motivations, fears, goals, and needs; ability to use self-understanding to regulate one's life; reflective nature
Naturalist (added in the 1990s)	Sensitivity to the environment and its elements; ability to see and/or appreciate patterns in nature and to draw on them effectively to solve problems
Moral (possible, not yet confirmed)	Concern with or sensitivity to the rules, behaviors, and processes that govern humans; reverence for the sanctity of life in various contexts; well-developed sense of right and wrong and what benefits the greater good

Robert Sternberg's triarchic theory of intelligence proposes that individuals can process or interact with ideas through three modes or intelligences: analytical, practical, and creative. Table 7.2 lists and briefly describes Sternberg's three proposed intelligence areas. Although Sternberg sees value in enabling individuals to strengthen and capitalize on the intelligence(s) in which they are strongest, he cautions that successful people often work from a balanced state in which all three areas function effectively as needed for a given setting. While schools tend to emphasize analytical intelligence almost exclusively, Sternberg suggests that teachers would be wise to help students understand how each of the intelligences contributes to success and to help them develop comfort and competence in working in all three ways.

Table 7.2: Robert Sternberg's Proposed Intelligences

Intelligence	Description
Analytical	Sometimes called "schoolhouse intelligence." Stresses seeing how parts make up wholes, planning, and reflecting on ideas. These are the kinds of strengths around which many, if not most, school tasks are constructed.
Practical	Sometimes called "street smarts" or "contextual intelligence." Stresses recognizing how ideas work in the world as well as developing solutions to and solving real-world problems. This strength allows an individual to readily apply learning to authentic contexts and to rally others to work together to address needs.
Creative	Sometimes called "imaginative problem solving." Focuses on shaping the environment in ways that suit an individual's vision and needs. This strength allows an individual to readily generate new ideas and possibilities.

Culture

The majority of teachers in today's schools in the United States are Caucasian and grew up with a middle-class background. By contrast, the students those teachers work with come from an increasing number of non-Caucasian backgrounds, and many are from low-income homes. The result is a growing gap between "how we do school" and the ways that many of our students learn. Unless educators become more culturally aware and more culturally competent or proficient, our schools will fail increasing numbers of students.

Culture can be defined in many ways. One definition with strong implications for teaching and learning is that culture is a set of attitudes, values, norms, traditions, and goals that characterize a particular group. What that definition suggests is that our cultural backgrounds vary and that the variance has a great deal to do with how we experience a place like school and how we interact in it. Said simply, our culture shapes how we learn. When students are asked to learn in a context that is a cultural mismatch, their learning is likely to suffer.

Think about a classroom in which the teacher comes from a Western, middle-class background. This teacher will probably

- Emphasize the achievement of the individual over that of a group

- Value independence more than helpfulness

- Use praise rather than criticism as a motivator

- Stress the development of cognitive skills over social skills

- Prefer that a student express feelings rather than remain silent out of respect for authority

- Emphasize personal property more than sharing

- Assume that parents should take active roles in a student's academic success

It may then come as a surprise to this teacher to learn that students from a number of non-Western or non-Caucasian cultures may well be more comfortable in a classroom in which

- The group is valued more than the individual

- Students can collaborate and be helpful

- Criticism is used as a vehicle for improvement

- Students are especially confident of their social skills

- Students remain silent as a way of expressing respect

- Students share resources as a group rather than have them assigned to individuals

Further, this teacher may be surprised to learn that in many students' homes, taking an active role in a child's education is seen as disrespectful to the teacher (Trumbull, Rothstein-Fisch, Greenfield, & Quiroz, 2001).

Increasingly, educators are coming to understand that cultural competence or cultural relevance is fundamental to teacher and learner success in contemporary classrooms. Culture is a significant component of an individual's mindset, and we already know from chapter 2 how strongly mindset influences teaching and learning. In other words, we are learning that culture is a dominant force in people's lives and that we need to teach with an awareness and an appreciation of cultural variance and in ways that affirm and draw on all the cultures of our students.

There is a paradox in culturally responsive teaching: although different cultures approach learning in different ways, it is not possible to generalize to a culture. That is, there are some learning preferences that characterize Latino cultures, but not all Latino students will behave according to those preferences. There are some learning preferences that are common to African American students, but not all African American learners will manifest those preferences. The same is true of French, Hmong, and Chinese students and students from any other culture. There are cultural patterns and individual variance within those patterns.

Figure 7.1 (page 144) presents six continua of cultural tendencies and beliefs that influence learning preferences. It is worthwhile for teachers to think about their own preferences and to place themselves on each continuum. It is also useful to reflect on the fact that some experts indicate that those who have grown up in the United States are often much further to the left on each continuum than are those who have grown up in Africa, China, Mexico, Russia, Southeast Asia, Japan, and the Middle East. In some instances, the cultures of the United Kingdom and Germany reflect similar preferences to those that typify the United States; in others, even those two cultures diverge markedly from U.S. patterns.

As teachers become more culturally proficient and their teaching becomes more relevant to students from a wide variety of backgrounds, they understand and demonstrate an understanding of the following principles:

- Diversity both between and within cultures is broad.

- When students are confident of their importance in the classroom community, they are more successful.

- People identify with groups that are important to them, and it is impossible to affirm the worth and dignity of an individual without also affirming the worth and dignity of the groups that matter to them.

- There are many ways to achieve a common learning goal, and teachers who are effective with a broad array of learners provide multiple avenues and support systems for success.

- Students' backgrounds are important in helping them develop a context for, and connection to, important new concepts and skills.

- Learning tasks must be relevant and engaging to the students asked to complete them (Ladson-Billings, 1994; Robins, Lindsey, Lindsey, & Terrell, 2002).

Gender

Just as culture influences student learning, so does gender, and just as students have culture-based learning preferences, they also have gender-based preferences. Just as it is critical for teachers to know that individual variance exists within cultural learning patterns, they must be aware that not all males adhere to learning patterns associated with males and not all females adhere to learning patterns associated with females. Nonetheless, understanding gender-based learning preferences should be very useful to teachers, many of whom, especially in the early years of school, are female and may favor approaches to learning that are associated with females—to the detriment of most males (and perhaps some females) in their classes.

Figure 7.1: Continua of cultural tendencies and beliefs.

Most experts who examine gender-associated learning differences and their impact on student achievement concur that boys and girls tend to "come at" learning in different ways—a conclusion that is not likely to surprise experienced teachers. While some of these experts emphasize the role of nature (including structures in the brain) in shaping these differences (for example,

Sax, 2005), others (for example, Eliot, 2009) emphasize the role of nurture (including societal and family expectations). One author draws what is probably the most common conclusion about this issue:

> The consensus holds that individuals are shaped both by nature and by nurture. Although biology is not destiny, it appears to set the outer bounds of performance in the absence of focused intervention. . . . Reasonable evidence suggests that social, experiential, and biological factors interact in many of the observed differences between females and males. (Salomone, 2003, p. 239)

Among gender-shaped learning differences are the following:

- Girls are more sensitive to sound than boys and therefore may be more distracted by classroom noise.

- Girls listen better than boys and thus may be more successful in classes heavy in lecturing.

- Boys are more attuned to motion than girls are, whereas girls are more likely to focus on objects and faces than boys are.

- Girls are more sensitive to a range of bright colors than boys are.

- Girls are more able to talk about feelings than boys are.

- Boys engage in physically riskier action than girls, perhaps because boys tend to overestimate their physical skills, while girls underestimate theirs.

- Girls are more likely than boys to try to affiliate with their teachers, to take their teachers' opinions and feedback seriously, to ask for help and advice from teachers, and to assume teachers are on their side.

- Girls are more likely than boys to do homework so that their teacher will be pleased. Boys are less likely to do homework unless it interests them.

- Girls enjoy being together to share ideas, secrets, and experiences. Boys enjoy being together around shared interests.

- Conversations are central to girls' friendships. Action is central to boys' friendships.

- Boys are more attracted to competition; girls, to collaboration.

- Boys may learn better in somewhat stressful contexts. That is less likely to be the case for girls.

- Boys are more adept at spatial and (some) number-based tasks. Girls are better at verbally based tasks.

- Boys are more likely to read nonfiction than girls and to prefer books that involve action and struggle. Girls do better than boys with fiction and tasks that relate to motives, behaviors, and reasons for actions (Salomone, 2003; Sax, 2005; Eliot, 2009).

Again, experts in the impacts of gender on learning remind us that it is unwise to generalize these patterns to all students of the same gender. Further, gender differences vary in degree and importance with a learner's age. The experts differ to some measure as to whether it is wiser to encourage students to work in ways that seem less gender-friendly, in order to extend their capacities and to compensate for disadvantageous patterns of socialization, or to encourage them to work predominantly in ways that seem "natural."

It is important to remember that the four elements that have an impact on learning profile (learning styles, intelligence preferences, culture, and gender) interact. Therefore, for example, males from one culture may approach learning somewhat differently from males from another culture. It's neither wise nor feasible to try to reduce an individual to a particular learning-profile label!

Learning Profile: An Evolving Concept

Clearly, the concept of learning profile is complex in terms of scope, reach, and grounding. Of the three broad areas related to learner variance—readiness, interest, and learning profile—learning profile and its four aspects are the most controversial among experts. The arguments are particularly heated in the areas of learning style and intelligence preference (also sometimes called *cognitive style*).

As we have noted, some highly respected researchers, among them Howard Gardner and Robert Sternberg, argue vigorously for the existence of cognitive styles, or intelligence preferences. At the same time, other noted psychologists (such as Linda Gottfredson at the University of Delaware and Daniel Willingham at the University of Virginia) argue with equal fervor that the construct of cognitive style or intelligence preference is ill informed and makes little sense in terms of learning. In addition, while some models of learning profile have been researched extensively (for example, the work of Rita and Kenneth Dunn and the work of Robert Sternberg), there is little research to support some other learning-profile models. Even the models that have been researched more extensively suffer from the fact that the research was largely conducted by the authors of the models and not replicated by other researchers. While it is not a fault that researchers study their own models, favorable research findings are often considered more robust when they have been replicated by those not directly invested in a model.

The term *learning style* itself suffers from vagueness because over the years it has often been applied to different conceptual models. Some researchers in this area contend that instead of learning style, we should be looking at the separate entities *cognitive style* and *learning strategy* (Gardner, 2006; Sadler-Smith, 2001). Cognitive style describes the consistent differences among individuals in organizing and processing information. These style differences are stable over time, automatic, and independent of intelligence. Learning strategy refers to the interface between cognitive style and the many factors present in the external learning environment (Riding & Rayner, 1997).

What Neuroscience Research Says About Learning Profile

Learning profile obviously concerns processes that occur in the brain. Yet neuroscientific research has discovered limited evidence to support the idea that individuals actually learn in different ways by using different neural networks to accomplish similar learning tasks. But there is *some* evidence, mostly related to gender. Studies have shown, for example, that female brains generally use more brain regions to process language than male brains and that the female advantage in language processing results from greater communication between the cerebral hemispheres (Garn, Allen, & Larsen, 2009; Schmithorst & Holland, 2007; Shaywitz et al., 1995; Wilke, Holland, & Krägeloh-Mann, 2007). In figure 7.2, the solid white areas show activation in a male brain and a female brain during language processing. Note the greater activation in the female brain. Other brain-imaging studies have shown that during mathematical processing, the brain areas activated in males are different from those activated in females (Keller & Menon, 2009).

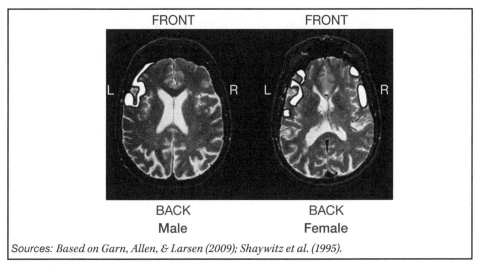

Sources: Based on Garn, Allen, & Larsen (2009); Shaywitz et al. (1995).

Figure 7.2: Areas activated during language processing.

Studies using electroencephalograms (EEGs) have shown that the activated brain regions differ among individuals of the same gender when performing the same cognitive task, suggesting that the EEGs are measuring different cognitive (that is, processing) styles (Goode, Goddard, & Pascual-Leone, 2002; McKay, Fischler, & Dunn, 2002; Okuhata, Okazaki, & Maekawa, 2009). As for learning strategies, the restrictive environments necessary for using

> Cognitive style describes consistent differences among individuals in organizing and processing information. Learning strategy refers to the interface of cognitive style with the external environment.

fMRI and EEG make it difficult for researchers to moderate and assess the environmental variables associated with learning-style models. On the other hand, thousands of research articles exist that have examined *behavioral* differences among individuals under varying environmental conditions.

What Learning Profile Should and Shouldn't Mean

Despite the controversies, when people think about their own learning experiences and watch their children or colleagues or students as they learn, they generally conclude that different people approach learning differently. We may not yet know quite how learning preferences work, or even why they do. What we do know, however, is that a one-size-fits-all approach to how people learn tends to be as unsatisfactory as a one-size-fits-all approach to readiness.

A fair statement about our current state of knowledge related to learning profile is that people seem to benefit from a range of approaches to teaching and learning. That is true on both the individual and group levels. In other words, within a classroom, some students would probably fare better with one approach to understanding how fractions work and other students would grasp the concept better with another approach. Even individuals, however, learn different things in different ways at different times.

In the face of ambiguities about various aspects of learning profile, how can a teacher reasonably address student differences in preferred ways to learn? How should—and shouldn't—teachers interpret and apply the construct of learning profile? Table 7.3 makes some general recommendations that seem warranted based on what we know about learning profile and what we do not yet know.

In the end, we have little evidence that trying to tag or label a student as a specific kind of learner is beneficial. Rather, a teacher who understands the current state of the art and the research related to learning preferences is likely to say, "How can I create a classroom that supports multiple ways to learn? How can I add variety to my teaching? And how can I help my students develop both a repertoire of approaches to learning and the self-awareness to know when an approach is working for them and when to change that approach?"

Some Guidelines for Differentiating in Response to Learning Profile

As was the case with the guidelines for responding to student variability in readiness and interest, those for attending to differences in learning profile will sound familiar because virtually all aspects of effective teaching are rooted in common principles and practices. Here are a few suggestions for thinking about and planning for learning-profile variation in a classroom:

Table 7.3: Recommendations for Practices Related to Learning Profile

Less Defensible Practice	More Defensible Practice
Ignoring or minimizing the importance of student differences in learning	Being aware of and studying differences in how individual students approach learning
Assessing students for learning-profile preferences and using the information to assign them to categories (for example, telling a student she is a visual learner and assigning tasks accordingly)	Helping students develop awareness of the ways people approach learning and of the particular approaches to learning that do and do not work for them as individuals
Assigning students to work regularly in their weaker modes or modes that are uncomfortable for them	Providing opportunities for students to work often in modes that are comfortable as well as occasionally asking them to try a new approach
Sticking with modes of teaching and learning that are comfortable for the teacher	Teaching in a variety of modes and offering varied approaches to learning as often as possible to make room for a variety of student learning preferences
Assuming a student will be consistent in learning preferences across subjects, topics, and times of day and year	Understanding that effective learners will draw on a variety of strategies, depending on the subject, the learner's comfort with a particular topic or skill, and the time of day and year

- Develop a set of learning-profile continua that you think represent your students' varied backgrounds and needs. Use this set to help you keep studying your students and to plan instruction. Figure 7.3 (page 150) shows a sample set of learning-profile continua a teacher can use for observation, planning, and conversations with students.

- Identify and articulate in student language what students should know, understand, and be able to do as a result of the unit of study you will be differentiating. Conveying this information ensures that you and your students are clear about the destination everyone is expected to reach. Including a variety of approaches to learning profile in teaching and learning plans ensures that more students arrive at the destination more efficiently.

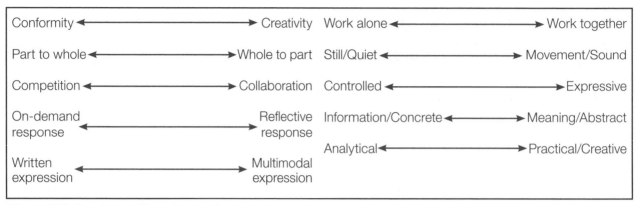

Figure 7.3: Continua of learning preferences.

- Consider using a preassessment of student learning preferences. Such surveys can be in the form of a checklist or a questionnaire. They can be stand-alone assessments or part of a broader preassessment of interests and school experiences. Young students or students who struggle with reading or writing find it helpful if they can respond to icons or images rather than words, if they can audio-record answers, or if they can give answers verbally and have someone else write them down. The preassessment can take place early in the school year or at the outset of a new unit of study. The purpose of a learning-profile survey is *not* to label students but rather to help them think about what makes learning work best for them and what does not work so well. Figure 7.4 provides a sample of a learning-profile preassessment.

- Find time in class to talk about your experiences as a learner—what works to help you learn and what slows you down. Ask students to reflect on how particular approaches to learning in class and at home do or do not help them succeed.

- Be sure to help students develop an awareness of and appreciation for varied perspectives on issues and varied approaches to solving problems in the classroom. Help them become aware of the ways in which culture and gender can shape our views and actions.

- Based on preassessment information and other knowledge about your students as a class, put into your lesson plans various ways of presenting information to students, various ways for students to explore ideas and use skills, and various ways for them to show what they have learned.

- Remember the connection between readiness and learning profile. While a particular approach to learning may help students work more efficiently, it is still true that they will not grow when tasks are well above or below their current level of functioning. Materials, directions, models, and expectations need to be just above a

Name:

Directions: Take a few minutes to write me a letter or an email that will help me understand how you think you learn best. You can draw pictures too if you would like to, and write about them instead of the letter or email. You can also say your answers on the audio-recorder if you would like that better.

Here are some things you could write or draw about or say. But it's okay if you have other things in mind. Remember, what I want to know is what to do to help you learn well.

1. Tell about a time when you learned something really well. It might be swimming or skating or drawing or reading or math or something else. What helped you learn then?

2. What are the top three things in a classroom that you like because they help you learn?

3. Do you like reading best, or do you like it best when the teacher (or someone else) reads to you? Do you like to draw what you know, or would you rather write about it? Do you like to work alone or with a partner? Do you like to be told just how to do something, or do you like making some choices yourself?

4. Tell about a time when something made it really hard for you to learn. That might have been a time at home or at school or somewhere else.

5. What else do you want me to know about what helps you learn?

Figure 7.4: A learning profile preassessment for a third-grade class.

student's current level of functioning, and supports or scaffolding are necessary to help students succeed at the new level of challenge.

- Be sure that plans for the flexible grouping of students include learning-profile groups. Some of these groups should be made up of students with similar approaches to learning, and others should include students with varied learning profiles, who will be helped to extend their understanding of content by seeing different perspectives on what they are studying.

■ Be sure that directions, rubrics, and models that support student work keep students focused on the lesson's essential knowledge, understanding, and skills. Remember that in the vast majority of instances, learning profile–based options should help students reach or exceed common KUDs. Assignments that are differentiated based on learning preferences should typically create alternate paths to the same destination.

■ Think about classroom procedures and routines that need to be in place for the learning profile–based options to work as they should. Then, make sure that students are ready to participate successfully in those routines. (See chapter 8.)

■ Get students up and moving around the classroom on a regular basis. This movement increases blood flow to the brain and stimulates long-term memory sites, making cognitive processing more efficient and successful.

■ As students work independently on learning profile–based tasks and applications, use your time to meet with individuals and small groups of students, monitoring progress, coaching for success, and noting what you learn so that your understanding of student strengths and needs grows consistently.

■ Continue to study your students and elicit their input on learning profile–based approaches that they find helpful in mastering essential content and on ways they would fine-tune current approaches. Ask them to suggest additional learning profile–based ideas.

■ Seek input from students on how they are feeling about their proficiency with essential knowledge, understanding, and skills.

> Assignments that are differentiated based on learning preferences should create alternate paths to the same destination.

■ Keep studying your content to understand various ways in which you can present, and students can explore and express, essential knowledge, ideas, and skills to maximize student success.

Exercise 7.1 (page 162) offers a checklist for reflecting on teacher practice in addressing student learning profile.

Differentiating Content, Process, and Product Based on Learning Profile

Thinking systematically about differentiating the three key classroom elements—content, process, and product—based on learning profile clarifies when and how to modify approaches to teaching and learning to benefit students.

Content

As explained in previous chapters, differentiating content can mean differentiating what students need to learn or differentiating how they gain access to what they need to learn. Continuing with the premise that teachers will more often want to differentiate routes of access rather than the core content itself, the teacher becomes a particularly important element in differentiating content. That is true because the teacher is often a key source of content for students. So *how* the teacher teaches can have a significant impact on the degree to which students with different learning profiles learn.

Here is a further explanation of what we mean. Quick, finish the following sentence: "Teachers tend to teach the way they . . ." Did you say, "were taught"? That is a very common response but not really accurate. Teachers tend to teach the way they *learn*. Their learning profile drives their teaching style. So students whose learning profiles are similar to that of the teacher will feel very comfortable in the learning situation, while those whose profiles are significantly different may have varying degrees of difficulty.

> A teacher's learning profile drives that teacher's teaching style.

We are *not* making the case for putting students and teachers with similar learning profiles in the same class. Several such experiments were attempted in the 1970s and 1980s with little or no success (Curry, 1990; Gregorc, 1979; Holland, 1982). Rather, we are suggesting that teachers be aware of their own learning profiles because those profiles most likely affect the decisions they make about which instructional strategies to use in their classroom. Therefore, it is essential for teachers to *extend* the ways in which they transfer knowledge to students, as well as to extend the avenues through which students access what they need to learn.

To differentiate content based on learning profile, teachers might do the following:

- Examine their own preferred modes of teaching to become aware of their tendencies to present in a particular format. For example, many secondary teachers lecture extensively. For some students, that does not present a problem. For students who are learning the language of the classroom, students who learn poorly by listening, students who do not hear well, students who have difficulty sitting still for long periods, students who lack a context for the content of the lecture, and others for whom that format is a poor fit, consistent oral presentation impedes access to important ideas and understandings.

- Expand the modes in which they present information to students to include visual presentations (pictures, video, diagrams, visual analogies, clips from movies or television, animations, and so on); auditory presentations (voice, music, podcasts, sounds from nature, and so on); demonstration; use of small-group dialogue and summary; and analytical, practical, and creative questions.

- Include whole-to-part teaching as well as part-to-whole teaching in most teacher presentations and reviews.

- Include analytical, creative, and practical elements in oral presentations so that students develop frameworks for understanding content (analytical), see how the ideas and skills are useful in the world beyond the classroom (practical), and learn how people look for and find innovative and effective solutions to problems related to the topic (creative).

- Examine their own culture- and/or gender-shaped views and approaches in order to become more aware of the ways in which their perspectives may be similar to or different from those of their students.

- Introduce perspectives from varied cultures and genders (by presenting examples, inviting experts, soliciting multiple student perspectives, and so on), with the intent of having students develop multifaceted thinking on important topics.

- Use podcasts or other recordings to give students the opportunity to review content that was covered in lectures.

- Use a variety of materials and illustrations that are likely to be gender-friendly for males and females.

- Provide graphic organizers or other written digests or organizers of oral teacher presentations to benefit students who learn better by reading than by listening.

- Use a variety of books on CD to reinforce key content for students who benefit from listening.

- Use a range of websites to illustrate how Web content is organized, how it works, and how it is used to benefit students who need to see rather than only hear.

- Use examples of important people in the discipline (contributors, problem solvers, innovators, newsmakers) who represent multiple cultures and both genders.

Some teachers may not be aware of the components of their own teaching style. A helpful technique for looking at your style is to put up a video camera at the back of your classroom, set the lens at wide-angle mode, and let it tape several lessons over several days. Then review the tape and examine your presentation style. Do you lecture more than necessary, or do you use a multimodal approach? Do you call on the girls, or the brighter students, or the quicker responders, or students on the right side of the room more than average? Do you walk around the room or tend to stand in one area? Do you smile often, call students by their names, and use humor (not sarcasm)? This analysis can help you determine what teaching techniques you may wish to alter and what new strategies you could implement to address a variety of student learning profiles.

Process

Process begins in earnest when students stop listening, watching, or reading and begin to work with the content in order to make sense of it for themselves. To differentiate process based on students' learning preferences, teachers might do the following:

- Provide a choice of working conditions for students (work alone, work in pairs, work in quads, work with the teacher).

- Call on students equitably so that students from all cultural, language, economic, and gender groups make consistent and valuable contributions to the class.

- Provide analytical, practical, and creative tasks that lead to the same essential outcomes.

- Provide varied modes of expression for student tasks (for example, give students the options of developing an annotated flow chart, a series of storyboards, or a well-organized paragraph to show the stages of the division of a cell).

- Encourage students to suggest other formats or modes of expression for their work.

- Provide places in a room where students who want to work quietly can be comfortable and another place where students who want to work together can talk quietly about their work. It can also be helpful to students who are very distracted by sounds to have headphones or earplugs to mute classroom noise.

- Provide carrels or a section in the room that has nothing on the wall, where students who are distracted by visual stimuli can work.

- Include both competitive and collaborative tasks in each unit, and allow students to select their options when appropriate.

- Have students play roles that require them to examine varied perspectives on issues, especially the perspective that is the opposite of what they accept.

- Develop tasks with a more concrete focus and tasks with a more abstract focus around the same learning goals and let students select their choice. It can also be useful to have some students work with one of the tasks, some with the other, and then ask them to work in pairs or teams to see how the two tasks make sense together.

Remember that when students explore learning through different modes, it is not the mode of exploration that should be the focus of feedback or grades. Rather, the essential content (KUDs) should be both the teacher's and the student's primary focus.

Product

Products are summative-type assessments that occur at the end of a unit or at a few critical points in a unit. Their purpose is to help students reveal what they know, understand, and can do related to the topic at hand. A product or summative assessment assignment is less effective when directions, modes of expression, time constraints, and other parameters get in the way of a student's ability to demonstrate competence. To differentiate products based on student learning profile, a teacher might do the following:

- Provide analytical, practical, and creative expression options that focus on the same essential outcomes.

- Provide varied modes of expression for student products.

- Allow students to suggest modes of expression for their products when appropriate.

- Provide competent models of student products in varied formats so that the class can see how students express core learning in varied modes or formats.

- Use recorded directions or read directions out loud for students who may not read well for various reasons but who could express key content in a nonprint format if they understood the directions.

- Be flexible with time parameters whenever possible for students who need more time to complete their work.

- Develop products and assessments that encourage students to express and defend varied perspectives on issues and to connect key content with their own experiences.

Remember that when students express learning through different modes, it is not the mode of exploration that should be the focus of feedback or grades. Rather, the essential content (KUDs) should be both the teacher's and the students' primary focus.

Differentiating With Synthesis Groups and Thinking Caps

This chapter has shown that teachers can attend to students' varied learning preferences in a classroom in numerous ways. We will take a closer look here at two commonly used strategies: synthesis groups and thinking caps. Both strategies can be adapted for use with a wide range of ages and subject-matter content. The main objective of these strategies is to focus students on meaning, understanding, and problem solving.

Synthesis Groups

When students have been working for a period of time (which might range from a class period or two, to a week or two, to a unit or longer), it is often effective for a teacher to ask them to reflect on what they have been learning—in other words, to answer the question "What is this really about?" or "Why does this matter?" This activity allows students to start to focus on the big picture or major conceptual scheme that is emerging rather than on factual details and isolated data. At such points, synthesis groups can be quite powerful. The following process generally works well for incorporating synthesis groups into the classroom:

- The teacher selects about four students who tend to approach learning or to express themselves in different ways.

- The group then has a specified amount of time to agree on the meaning of the content the class has been working on and to express that meaning in at least three different modes.

- The teacher does not tell the students which modes they must use, but it is helpful to put a list of possibilities on the board. The list might include such options as pantomime, visual analogy, musical analogy, sketch, model, cartoon, monologue, and collage. The options, of course, would vary with the age of the students and the time and materials available.

- Students may work independently or collaboratively to develop the three or more modes of expression, but the whole group must approve and, if necessary, modify the expressions before sharing them so that the presentations convey the meaning the group intended.

- Three useful criteria for students to use in developing their expressions are (1) the clarity of the essential ideas they have chosen to express, (2) the accuracy and appropriateness of those ideas to help classmates understand the content more deeply, and (3) the effectiveness of the mode of expression in conveying the essential ideas.

To make the best use of class time, the teacher should consider having two groups share their work with each other and select what they consider to be the most powerful example from each group. Then, the examples selected as most powerful (generally four or fewer) can be shared with the whole class for group discussion. Almost inevitably, students understand what matters most about the content more deeply and more broadly as a result of seeing ideas presented through various lenses.

Our first "In the Classroom" scenario is an example of using synthesis groups in an elementary classroom.

In the Classroom

Neighborhood Unit, Synthesis Groups (Elementary School)

The primary-grade students in Mr. Callison's classroom had been studying neighborhoods. A big idea the group had been exploring was that good neighbors work together to make the place they live better for everyone in it. The students had studied their own neighborhoods, heard about neighborhoods in the news, read stories about neighbors, and interviewed relatives about the neighborhoods they grew up in. As one culminating activity, Mr. Callison asked students to work together in groups of four to tell whether they believed the idea that good neighbors make good neighborhoods and to give evidence from what they had learned for their conclusion. He used his knowledge of students' varied expression strengths to form mixed learning-profile groups. Each group had to find at least three ways/modes of expression to argue for or against the idea. He put on the board a list of ten ways students could express their ideas, for example: sketches, an oral conversation, a list of dos and don'ts, cartoons, or a song. He also encouraged the students to come to him with other ideas for the list. No students in a group could use the same mode of expression. Every student in the group had to be able to explain every other student's conclusion and evidence for the conclusion. Each group would share its work in a small-group session with Mr. Callison and would select the work of one person in the group to share with the class as a whole.

Thinking Caps

In a modification of the Six Thinking Hats method developed by Edward de Bono (1985), this strategy asks students to consider an issue by putting on one of five "thinking caps." With younger students, it is a good idea to use paper or cardboard hats to remind them of their roles. It can be helpful for older students to have placards in front of them with caps of the color they are "wearing" at a given time.

In a thinking caps exercise, students consider a problem or issue that is open ended. For example, younger students might talk about what would happen if they solved problems the way a character in a story they have just read or heard solves them. Students in a middle school science class might discuss the implications of a new construction project on a local ecosystem so that they can take a stand with the city council. High school students in a government class might examine the feasibility of granting teenagers the same sorts of free speech rights that adults have.

During the discussion, students express opinions based on the particular cap they are wearing. The caps represent the following thinking styles:

- Blue cap—Values facts, information, data

- Yellow cap—Intuitive, trusts his or her feelings, is concerned about the feelings of others

- Green cap—Highly imaginative, creative, looks for innovative solutions

- Orange cap—Practical, wants to bring people together to solve the problem

- Red cap—Looks for problems and flaws (red flags) in suggestions, tends to be cautious

As the teacher or the students raise questions about the issue or problem, students respond to those questions and to one another's input from the perspective of the thinking cap they are wearing. The goal of the discussion is to reach a worthwhile conclusion, and participants should contribute to that goal in ways that move the group's thinking ahead.

There are several ways to organize this activity:

- Students may volunteer for the cap they think fits them best and remain in that role throughout the discussion. This approach lets students contribute through their strengths and allows the class to see contributions from multiple approaches to problem solving.

- Students may start with preferred roles and be asked to switch roles later in the discussion. This allows students to try out different perspectives on problems and may clarify for students where their own strengths are or help them discover benefits in less-familiar roles. The discussion may be limited to five students, each wearing a different cap, with other students serving as observers and respondents to the discussion.

- Every student in the class may have a cap to wear and may contribute to the discussion from the perspective of the cap color. In that instance, there might be four or five students with green caps, three or four with red caps, and so on.

In many real-world situations, productive thinking occurs when various individuals approach problems in various ways. Good solutions typically call for data and order, intuition, freewheeling ideas, caution, and so on. Different people bring different strengths to the process. Thinking caps can help students develop and understand their particular strengths as well as help them recognize and value the approaches others take to thinking.

Our second "In the Classroom" scenario is an example of using thinking caps in a high school classroom.

A Final Thought

We have devoted three separate chapters to differentiating instruction in response to student readiness, interest, and learning profile. Although this structure has allowed us to give some depth of attention to each of these aspects of responsive teaching, it might also suggest that teachers should differentiate for only one element at a time. In reality, of course, that approach would limit teachers' possibilities and students' opportunities. Teachers should think about at least two of the elements in planning for a single lesson. In planning for a unit, all three elements are certainly important.

In the Classroom

Pollution Unit, Thinking Caps (High School)

Mrs. Pappas had been working with her high school students on the topic of pollution in a unit on environmental science. She began by assigning students to "Think Tanks" that would work throughout the unit to develop a creative and effective proposal for reducing pollution in their community. The groups of five or six students met together several times during the unit to develop and refine their proposals as they learned more and more about the issues related to pollution. One strategy she taught the students for thinking carefully and creatively about their ideas was Thinking Caps. Each time members of a group felt they had arrived at a plan that was viable and innovative, they conducted a Thinking Caps discussion about the plan.

One student presented the plan to the group and took notes as group members discussed the plan based on the particular thinking cap they selected for the session. Students wrote their names on index cards in the color that represented the hat they would wear for the session, then folded the cards to serve as name placards and reminders to group members of the role they were playing in the discussion. The student wearing the blue cap contributed facts, information, and data relevant to the discussion. The student with the yellow cap injected feelings about both the content of the plan and the groups' work processes. The student with the green cap looked for ideas and approaches that were both novel and promising to improve aspects of the proposal. The student with the orange hat looked for ways to make the ideas practical and also for ways in which the group could work together more productively. The student with the red hat raised potential problems or concerns that various stakeholders in the community might have with the ideas. From time to time, Mrs. Pappas sat in on the Thinking Caps discussions of various groups and also debriefed with the class as a whole about the Thinking Caps process—including her observations as she watched the groups use the procedure and noted the students' reactions to it.

For example, a high school science teacher may be planning a lesson in which students will have practical, analytical, and creative options for responding to a lab experiment (differentiation for learning profile). At the same time, however, there may be several students in the class who struggle with academic vocabulary. The teacher plans to review key terms with those students just before they begin their lab responses (differentiation for readiness).

An elementary teacher may have all students reading biographies. Some students will need challenging books that are well above grade level, while others will need books that are below grade level (differentiation for readiness). At the same time, the teacher encourages students to select a biography that reflects something they like or want to learn about. Some students will choose to read about sports figures, some will choose scientists or doctors, and others will choose women who were social pioneers (differentiation for interest). When students share their reading with others, the teacher may decide to provide visual, written, and kinesthetic options for their presentations (differentiation for learning profile). As is true with many things in school, it is wise to think about students on multiple levels when planning for differentiation. Use all the tools necessary to build successful learning opportunities.

A Better Scenario

Ms. Powell is fascinated by history and wants her students to see themselves and their world in the events of the past. She gives lectures from time to time but takes care to involve the students in a variety of ways. She asks students to take turns keeping a ledger, in which they record key ideas from the presentations as well as details of assignments. Students can use the ledger in class to ensure that their notes and understandings of assignments are accurate. It is also very helpful for students who have been absent. In addition, Ms. Powell provides graphic organizers that follow the structure of the lecture for students who do better with that format. She sometimes completes the organizer herself on the board or on a screen so that students can see how she summarizes important information. She also makes a point of using many images to help students imagine what particular events might have looked like, and she has a large and growing collection of clips from movies, television, and the news that connect with important ideas from history.

Ms. Powell is careful to spotlight how different people and groups felt about historical events, both when they happened and after. She often reminds her students that history books would be written quite differently if the people who lost wars or who lacked power during a particular time period had written them. She points out the many ways that people explore, record, and challenge history. She provides varied options for the students themselves to explore, record, and challenge what they are learning. Her criteria for quality work are clear to the students, but they have a good bit of room to decide how they will present their work.

Bondi finds it interesting how often he sees himself in history this year. That was not the case last year. Samet is doing well in history because of the note-taking support and images Ms. Powell provides. As a result, he is contributing more in class and writing more as well. Elsbeth is enjoying writing in history much more this year. Ms. Powell insists that students' writing be organized and well supported, but she seems to understand that different students will achieve that goal in different ways. At first, Jake was a bit unnerved by the choices Ms. Powell offered. He had always been more comfortable with assignments that left little ambiguity about what the teacher wanted him to do. He has discovered this year, however, that he does fine with a variety of analytical approaches to learning, and Ms. Powell has helped him develop several ways of presenting his work that are proving useful in other classes as well.

Exercise 7.1

A Checklist for Differentiating Instruction Based on Student Learning Profile

Reflect on your curriculum for a unit, semester, or year, and then respond to the following questions. After you finish, review your responses and think about where you might modify your instructional practices to more effectively address your students' varied learning profiles. Building administrators can use this activity at a faculty meeting to discuss the school's progress in working toward differentiation in response to students' learning profiles. The questions could also provide a framework for planning professional development and for helping teachers incorporate learning-profile differentiation into their instructional plans.

1. Do you clearly articulate KUDs for units and for lessons?

2. Do you ensure that students are clear about KUDs as they work with learning-profile options so that their work focuses on what is essential about the lesson or unit?

3. Have you thought about how culture and gender influence your teaching and learning?

4. Do you understand the various cultural backgrounds of your students and adapt teaching and learning so that the classroom is a good fit for students from all backgrounds?

5. Have you accounted for the ways in which gender may affect your students' learning?

6. Have you developed a set of learning-profile options to use in planning and teaching?

7. Have you developed and administered a student learning-profile survey?

8. Do you use contemporary technologies as teaching and learning tools to help students learn through a variety of modalities and to extend your presentation approaches?

9. Do you use both similar and dissimilar learning profile–based groups as part of each unit?

Differentiation and the Brain • © 2011 Solution Tree Press • solution-tree.com

Visit **go.solution-tree.com/instruction** to download this page.

10. Do you provide a range of working arrangements in the classroom?

11. Do you provide learning profile–based work and practice options to students as appropriate, and do you invite them to propose learning profile–based options as well?

12. Do you provide learning profile–based product and assessment options to students, as appropriate?

13. Do you make environmental adaptations for students who need to move around, need quiet or sound to work, or may be distracted by movement or "busy" spaces?

14. Do you have a systematic way of recording observations of your students' learning preferences?

15. Do you use what you learn about student learning profiles to inform your instruction?

16. Do you consider critical readiness needs in planning learning profile–based assignments?

17. Do you make time to talk about how you have come to understand your own learning preferences and to approach learning in ways that work for you?

18. Do you help students understand what is working for them as learners, what is not, and how to adjust their approaches to learning to help them succeed?

19. Do you provide clear guidelines for work and quality when students are doing learning profile–based assignments so that they are prepared to succeed?

20. Have you developed classroom routines and procedures that support students in working with varied tasks and in varied group configurations?

21. Have you prepared students to work effectively with, and contribute to the refinement of, those routines?

22. Do you use student work time to meet with individuals and small groups about their work?

Possible Changes to Consider

CHAPTER 8

Managing a Differentiated Classroom

The greatest sign of success for a teacher is to be able to say, "The children are now working as if I did not exist."

—Maria Montessori

A teacher with the conscious goal of supporting the success of each learner will necessarily learn to use all available classroom elements flexibly so that there is "room" for a variety of students to flourish. The teacher will provide many opportunities for students to work in ways that work for them. This requires being flexible oneself and guiding students in working effectively with routines designed to permit both flexibility and predictability. For many teachers, the prospect of a classroom in which students may be doing a variety of things at a given moment is daunting. It seems more viable—and easier—to have everyone work in a sort of lockstep manner. It's just more comfortable for the teacher that way. However, the price for teacher comfort is often a classroom that makes room for only a portion of its learners.

A Common View of Classroom Management

For many teachers, their earliest professional anxieties focused not on whether they could generate worthy curriculum, whether they could use assessment to benefit student instruction, or whether they could create a learning environment that felt inviting to students. Rather, their first—and often dominant—anxiety was whether they could control their students. This anxiety takes its toll. A study conducted in the state of Washington to determine why teachers leave the profession revealed that 29 percent left because of difficulty in dealing with student discipline issues, but this number rose to 53 percent in high-poverty schools (Elfers, Plecki, & Knapp, 2006).

A Case in Point

Mrs. Carson's classroom is a "tight ship." At the beginning of the year, she makes sure that her students know that she expects them to be seated quietly, to stay at their desks throughout class unless they get permission from her to get up to sharpen a pencil or get materials, and to talk only when she calls on them. She reminds them that there are penalties for breaking those rules and that she is consistent in applying the penalties to any student who violates the rules. The students see that consistency early on, so her classes are orderly, and students follow instructions.

The school's principal is encouraging teachers to develop classrooms with flexible routines and procedures that allow attention to various learner needs. Mrs. Carson is not comfortable with a class where students are turned loose to do whatever they want, so she has resisted his requests to differentiate instruction. At some point, however, the principal tells her he will be coming to observe her class to see how she is addressing her students' different learning needs. She tries a differentiated task a few days before the observation so that the students will be "primed" for his visit.

The day of the "trial run," Mrs. Carson tells her students she is going to give them different work in class that day and reminds them that she will enforce her rules about being out of desks and talking. She gives the directions for the two different tasks, tells each student where to sit in the room, and asks the students to move quietly to their new seats, which they do.

After that, however, things do not go so smoothly. Some students leave their materials at their original seats and can't go get them without teacher approval. Others do not understand the directions and have to wait while she moves around the room repeating the directions. That results in restlessness and talking, and she has to deduct points from many students' work. When the students finish their work, they are not sure what to do with their papers or what to do next. That leads to more restlessness, more talking, and more penalties. When the bell rings to dismiss class, the students leave the room with materials and chairs out of place.

Mrs. Carson tells the principal that her students are simply not mature enough to work unless she directs them as a group. She requests that he not come to observe her class because it is evident that differentiation can't work in her subject and with her students.

Most teachers, of course, do learn to keep order in the classroom, or they probably could not survive in the profession. Unfortunately, however, for many teachers, classroom management continues to be a control issue that, on some level, pits them against their students and leads to a sense that students are relatively untrustworthy in terms of self-management and generally incapable of directing their own work. In turn, those conclusions lead to many classrooms in which teachers exercise a sort of "frontal control"—a high level of teacher-centered, teacher-directed instruction. With that pattern as the norm, it is difficult to attend to the variety of learner needs in the classroom.

An Alternative View of Classroom Management

John Dewey (1938) reminded us that the ultimate goal of education is to produce students who exercise self-control and independence as learners. That outcome seems feasible only if we teach students the skills and attitudes that lead to independence, and far less so if their primary classroom experiences center on being controlled or managed. A more fruitful way of thinking about classroom management is *leading students* and *managing classroom routines.* Better still is leading students to be participants in creating a classroom that helps everyone become the best learner and person he or she can be. Table 8.1 contrasts the approaches of leaders and managers in the classroom.

Table 8.1: Approaches of Leaders and Managers

Leader	Manager
Focuses on *people*	Focuses on *mechanics*
Has a vision for something good	Plans schedules
Has the capacity to share the vision and enlist others in it	Handles details
Builds a team for achieving the vision	Prepares materials
Renews commitment to the vision	Arranges furniture
Celebrates successes	Orchestrates movement
	Practices routines
	Troubleshoots

Most adults bristle at being managed. In such circumstances, we feel manipulated and depersonalized, as though we were a problem to be solved rather than a person with a perspective and a voice. We often respond as less than our best selves. Students are not very different in that regard. On the other hand, in the presence of a leader who establishes a vision or a worthy goal and enlists our participation in achieving that goal, we are energized and cooperative. Again, students share these same human inclinations.

A teacher who aspires to create an effectively differentiated classroom learns to help students understand why such a classroom matters and then to join him or her in crafting a classroom that is efficient and effective for each of them. Certainly such classrooms present elements that teachers must manage, but the feeling is much different than in a classroom in which the teacher manages students and does so from a position of mistrust.

Interestingly, researchers find that there are also intellectual benefits to classrooms that operate flexibly. Knapp, Shields, and Turnbull (1992) report that there are essentially four kinds of classroom environments that stem from teacher management beliefs and styles:

1. Dysfunctional learning environments—In these classes, the teacher and students constantly struggle for control. The feeling is uneasy, and carrying on sustained academic work is difficult because of the underlying power struggle.

2. Adequate learning environments—Here, a basic level of order allows the class to accomplish some academic work. However, there is still significant tension stemming from a power struggle, and interruptions are common.

3. Orderly-restrictive learning environments—These classes run smoothly and are highly managed. Routines are tight, and the teacher uses a limited range of instructional strategies.

4. Orderly-flexible learning environments—These classes also run smoothly. However, they are characterized by looser (but not loose) structures. Teachers use a much wider range of instructional strategies and classroom routines.

The orderly-flexible classrooms are the ones most likely to focus on meaning and understanding, and the reason is straightforward. Learners have to grapple with ideas, try them out, make mistakes, and dispel misunderstandings if they are to really grasp and own what we ask them to learn. Those acts require time, space, experimentation, and collaboration. They are impossible in the first two types of environments and nearly so in "tight ship" classrooms. When teachers are comfortable managing only routine and lower-level types of tasks, they tend to turn to the more passive teaching and learning approaches that effectively limit what students can learn. That is, such teachers "'teach defensively,' choosing methods of presentation and evaluation that simplify content and reduce demands on students in return for classroom order and minimal student compliance on assignments" (Darling-Hammond, Bransford, LePage, & Hammerness, 2005, p. 331).

Flexible learning environments are brain-friendly. They encourage students to enter into what Renate Caine and Geoffrey Caine refer to as a state of *relaxed alertness* (Caine, Caine, McClintic, & Klimek, 2005). This optimal emotional state emerges in learning situations that consist of low threat and high challenge, so that the learner feels confident and competent while being intrinsically motivated. In this environment, the learner is both relaxed and emotionally engaged in the learning and is willing to take risks in questioning, experimenting, and higher-order thinking. Furthermore, orderly and flexible environments encourage communication through teacher and peer questioning and feedback. These discussions help students to identify critical information and concepts, to think more deeply, to analyze situations, to make important decisions, and to communicate their understandings to others. All of these actions develop the brain's executive functions and contribute to establishing the cerebral networks required to remember what was learned.

Other research findings in cognitive neuroscience support the idea that students who have flexibility in their learning environments show increased competence over students in more traditional environments. For example, one semilongitudinal study was conducted during two consecutive years with 210 children in elementary schools with traditional and flexible instructional approaches. The results showed a greater increase in the creative performance of the children in the flexible classrooms from year one to year two compared to those in the traditional setting (Besançon & Lubart, 2008). Another study showed that flexible learning environments significantly improved the young students' learning of new vocabulary words (Colunga & Smith, 2008).

Problem-solving performance also appears to improve in flexible learning environments. In a study involving students interacting with technology, allowing students the flexibility to pursue case studies to solve problems resulted in higher achievement than having students simply follow the information presented by the teacher. The study showed that it is possible to improve individual learning in a technology environment by using questioning strategies that trigger students to activate their higher cognitive processes as they study the contextually rich material of the cases they choose (Demetriadis, Papadopoulos, Stamelos, & Fischer, 2008).

Teachers, too, are likely to pursue the development of their own knowledge and skills when they work in a school that supports flexible learning environments (Tynjälä, 2008). From the standpoint of the nonnegotiables of effective differentiation featured in this book, orderly-flexible classrooms are necessary to support the following:

- A growth mindset on the teacher's part—that is, a belief that each student in the class can and will learn what is necessary for success, including skills of productive and increasingly independent work

- Respect for individuals—that is, the belief that students give their best when it feels rewarding to do so

- The belief that each student is worthy of high-quality curriculum with a clear focus on student understanding—that is, an unwillingness to be content with remediating some students or having some students consistently engage with low-level tasks while others are deemed able to reason and solve problems

- A determination to do whatever it takes to support student success—that is, an understanding that one-size-fits-all approaches are too narrow for student needs and a willingness to provide materials, timelines, support systems, strategies, student groupings, and routines that will get the job done for each learner

While teachers may fear that a differentiated or flexibly run classroom is an invitation to chaos, that is not and cannot be the case. Substantive learning can occur only in an orderly context. The goal in managing a differentiated classroom is to create order that supports flexibility, not order that supports rigidity. In other words, a well-planned differentiated classroom centered around a positive learning environment and a growth mindset is one of the best "disciplinary" tools there is.

Effective differentiation, then, requires that a teacher learn the skills of flexible classroom management. The good news is that virtually all teachers can learn these skills. Many teachers do not come by them automatically or even naturally. However, they are not complex and can, like most things, be learned with conscious intent. The payoff for students when their teachers become confident in guiding flexible classrooms is increased engagement with learning and increased achievement. The payoff for teachers is an enhanced sense of professional efficacy. The remainder of this chapter focuses on some key principles and strategies for leading students and managing classroom elements in a way that strikes the optimal balance between order and flexibility.

> The goal in managing a differentiated classroom is to create order that supports flexibility, not order that supports rigidity.

Seven Principles of Leading Students

Teachers who adhere to and enact seven basic principles will necessarily become leaders of their students. The principles enter the classroom with the teacher on the first day of school and are central to the teacher's thinking, decision making, planning, and actions throughout the year. Some of these principles will sound familiar from earlier in the book. However, it is important to revisit them briefly here to demonstrate how teacher beliefs and classroom elements intertwine to form a coherent classroom system.

1. Every student in the classroom is important and worthy of respect. Recognizing that teaching is fundamentally about building lives (Tompkins, 1996), the teacher is consistently conscious of the value of each life and consistently seeks to dignify each student in individual interactions and in front of the group as a whole.

2. A classroom environment that maximizes student potential reflects high regard for the individuals in it, high challenge, and high support. Classroom environments that support the hard work and risk of learning begin with positive and growing connections between the teacher and each student, leading to a clear sense of team or community among members of the class.

3. Every student in the class should have access to high-quality curriculum. The teacher's job is to ensure that every student works with and masters essential knowledge, understanding, and skills at a level that enables the student to retain, apply, and transfer what is

essential in the content. Therefore, the teacher works to ensure that each student regularly engages with curriculum that is inviting and that calls on the student to understand and reason.

4. Students in a given class will differ in readiness, interest, and learning profile in ways that affect learning. Those differences are influenced by a variety of factors and are both normal and valuable. Students learn best when teaching accounts for their various readiness levels, particular interests, and preferred ways of learning.

5. The teacher's job is to study the differences and to respond to them in ways that maximize student growth. Understanding students' evolving learning needs is as central to a teacher's success as understanding the content to be taught.

6. The classroom belongs to everyone in it in terms of both opportunity and responsibility. Making the classroom work for everyone will require contributions from everyone.

7. Teacher and students alike should have a shared vision of a classroom that works for everyone. As the architect of the vision, the teacher must lead the students in understanding, appreciating, refining, extending, implementing, and evaluating the vision.

Developing a classroom that reflects these principles is always a work in progress for both teacher and students. They are co-learners, building a learning place for each person in their classroom community. When a teacher enacts the principles, he or she is highly likely to become a leader of students rather than merely a manager of them.

Beginning to Lead

Students may not be accustomed to differentiated classrooms or orderly-flexible environments. If that is the case, the teacher must set a tone and a direction at the outset of the year that will help students recognize and reflect on how this class is, or could be, different and more effective. Certainly the teacher will renew his or her commitment to working from a growth or fluid mindset, regularly asking the question "Which of my thoughts and actions signal my belief that each student can and will learn what matters most, and which do not?" The teacher, too, will make every effort to connect with and to signal an interest and belief in each learner.

There are a number of ways in which teachers can form positive links with learners as a school year begins:

- Learning students' names before the year begins, or very quickly after students arrive

- Being sure to pronounce names correctly and using appropriate nicknames students prefer

- Using interest, learning-profile, and other surveys to find out about students as individuals

- Acting on information provided by student surveys

- Standing at the door to speak briefly with students as they come into and leave the classroom

- Using only positive humor (not sarcasm) in the classroom and laughing together

- Paying positive attention to students who are often overlooked or subjects of negative attention

- Sharing a vision for a class that works for everyone

- Asking students to help develop class rules/guidelines/procedures

- Acknowledging both privately and in front of the class significant student or group contributions to the success of a task or class (ensuring that students who are generally not recognized positively are spotlighted when appropriate)

- Using morning or afternoon meetings with younger students to begin or end the day with a student focus

- Taking a few minutes in class to share teacher stories and experiences with students

- Taking a few minutes in class for students to share their stories

- Using personal journals in which students can communicate with teachers

- Asking students to assist in the classroom

- Learning about students' cultures and including them in the curriculum

- Using examples from books, music, sports, and hobbies that kids care about to illustrate important class content

- Having places in the classroom to display student work and artifacts that students enjoy

- Acknowledging students' birthdays

- Attending extracurricular events that are important to students

- Acknowledging students through quick individual conversations as they are doing classwork

- Calling or emailing parents with good news

- Checking to make sure that students have what they need to succeed

- Determining what stretches or challenges individual students and expressing appreciation when they accept and persist with the challenge

In the very earliest days of the school year, teachers who are leaders of students will begin to involve them in thinking about how the classroom should work so that each student will have a strong school year. Generally, teachers will conduct brief conversations with students over several days rather than spend large blocks of time at once on these discussions. The topics might follow this progression:

- Who are you as individuals? Who are we as a class?

- Does it seem that we are alike in our interests and needs and strengths?

- What kind of class would it take for all of us to be able to learn efficiently and effectively?

- What sorts of rules, routines, and ways of working will be necessary to have a classroom in which each of us succeeds as a learner?

Such efforts can have a welcome outcome. Since the early 2000s, neuroscientists have focused on the social components of brain development and how they affect behavior. Much of this focus has been on children and adolescents, and particularly on the relationships they build with peers, teachers, and others (Ochsner, 2007). So it is not surprising that educational researchers have found that the single most important factor in classroom management is the development of a positive relationship between the student and the teacher (Hall & Hall, 2003). For example, Marzano, Marzano, and Pickering (2003) completed an analysis of one hundred studies on classroom management and found that the quality of teacher-student relationships was the most important factor in all aspects of classroom management. Bender (2003) argued that a positive relationship is the basis of all effective discipline and encouraged educators to consider the impact of any single disciplinary strategy on the long-term relationship they have with their students. Stipek (2006) emphasized that teachers should focus directly on their relationships with the students in the class but cautioned that teachers should not compromise on holding students accountable for their behavior.

Ferguson (2002) used a survey technique to inquire about disciplinary matters among a group of secondary students. The results indicated that students preferred to have positive relationships with their teachers and that African American students, in particular, were highly responsive to teachers who showed that they cared about the students' learning and lives. Clearly, there is a convergence among the researchers that a positive teacher-student relationship is the very basis of effective classroom management and that in the absence of such a relationship, effective classroom management will be difficult.

Strategies for Helping Students Examine Their Learning Differences

There are many strategies for helping students in a class see that they are not a matched set in terms of their learning strengths and needs. Once they have examined their learning differences, the teacher can proceed to raise the question of what kind of class could be effective for everyone. Here are four strategies, with explanations of how to implement them. The teacher should make appropriate adjustments for the students' grade level.

Graphing Your Strengths

Early in the school year, give students a blank graph whose horizontal axis contains several aspects of the subject(s) you will be teaching them and whose vertical axis contains either pictures or descriptors in student language indicating how good the student feels his or her performance is in that area. Have students add two to four more areas to the horizontal axis that they would like to tell about. Ask students to graph their strengths as they see them at that time. Graph yourself for the students first, both to demonstrate the assignment and to let the students learn a bit about you. Figure 8.1 shows a third-grader's graph of his relative strengths. The students had been instructed to use the smiley faces to show how good they thought they were in eight areas that the teacher had put on the horizontal axis of the graph and to add and rate two or three more areas they wanted to share about themselves.

Students can present one or two items from their graphs to the class. Post all graphs on the walls. Have students look for patterns that can complete the sentence "In general, it is true that . . ." Ask students to discuss the patterns they saw. They inevitably conclude that each student has highs and lows and that no one is the same in every aspect of the class.

Try It On for Size

Ask a small student to try on a very large jacket and a large student to try on a very small one. (Be sure to select students who enjoy being the center of attention.) Ask how the clothes feel, how the students would feel after wearing them for a day, and how they would feel after wearing them for a year. Ask students to connect the activity with their class.

A Visit to the Doctor

Give role-play cards to pairs of students. One student is the parent; the other is the child. You are the physician. Each role-play card specifies a different malady and outlines what the parent and child should say to the physician.

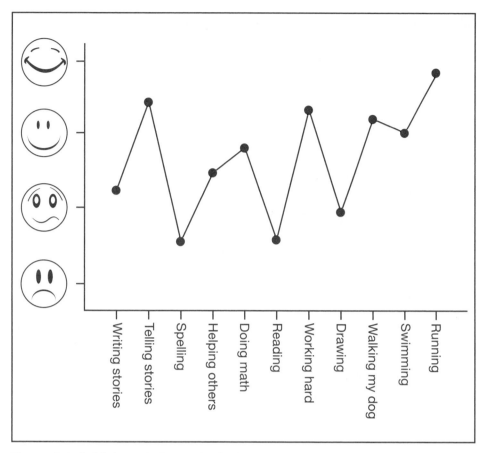

Figure 8.1: A third-grader's graph of relative strengths.

No matter the problem, the physician prescribes cold medicine. Only the final student has a cold.

Ask students to connect the activity with their class.

Paper People

Provide students with cutouts of a person (about ten inches tall), as well as stripes, dots, pants, and so on. Give a series of directions that students will follow to show how they like to learn. For example: If you are a girl, use short pants; if you are a boy, use long pants. If you like math best, make a green shirt; if you like science best, make a yellow shirt; if you like reading best, make a blue shirt; if you like social studies best, make an orange shirt. If you like to work alone, put stripes on your shirt; if you like to work with a partner, put dots on your shirt; if you like working in groups, put zigzags on your shirt. If you learn best by listening, make your shoes white; if you learn best by reading, make your shoes red; if you learn best by doing things, make your shoes blue (and so on).

Students put their finished figures on a bulletin board. Ask students to find figures that are just alike. (There are usually few or none.)

Helping Students Think About Differentiation

Once the students have become more aware of their learning differences, the teacher should probably guide them in developing broad descriptors of what their class would need to be like if it were a fit for everyone. Students often reach the following conclusions:

- Students might not always need the same amount of time to complete work.

- Students might need or want to read different things.

- They might need to learn things in different ways.

- Different groups might be working on different things at the same time.

- It might be helpful if students could express what they learn in different ways.

- The teacher might need to meet with or teach small groups of students or individual students to make sure everyone is learning what he or she needs.

- Students will be able to help one another sometimes because of their different strengths.

- The teacher might need to teach in different ways to make sure that everyone learns.

The teacher should feel free to pose questions that will help students consider angles they may not have thought about. For example:

- If you are working in groups, how will those groups need to function to be effective?

- What guidelines should we establish for effective work with partners and groups so that we all understand what we need to do in a group?

- What does it mean to be an effective colleague? What should you do (and not do) when a classmate asks you for help?

- If I am working with a group of students, what will happen if everyone comes to me with their questions?

- What are some ways we can be sure help is available when I am working with a group or individual and am off limits for questions?

- What will we need to do to ensure that the classroom is organized and orderly so that it will not be a problem when we have several things happening at once in the room?

As the teacher begins to differentiate instruction, it is important for everyone in the class to have fundamental understandings of why the class is operating as it is and how it should proceed. In addition, the teacher should return throughout the year to brief conversations about the understandings to review, add, and refine classroom routines and procedures. The teacher also needs to ask students to evaluate how the class is going, using the understandings as a yardstick, and to ask the students for suggestions when things are not going as smoothly as they ought to be. In a relatively short span of time, students should have both understanding of and ownership in the class so that they can articulate to parents, guests in the room, and other students why the class is differentiated. Here are some examples of statements that demonstrate student understanding of why differentiation is important:

- Because we do not all learn alike

- Because we have different strengths and weaknesses

- Because each of us needs to build on our strengths and figure out how to handle our weaknesses

- Because we like different things

- Because we have different talents

- Because we all need to grow, and we have to grow from where we are

It is also wise for a teacher to address questions or concerns students are likely to have as they begin to work in a differentiated classroom and to do so before the students have to spend much time wondering about them. For example, a teacher might explain that tomorrow, students in two groups will be working with a video camera (or on the computer, or with calligraphy pens, or whatever students might find interesting or attractive) and other groups will not. She might say that she knows that other students will be wondering when they will have a turn with that equipment and reassure them that everyone will have a chance to work with it sometime during the first marking period. The goal is to let students know that the teacher is aware of the things students find appealing and already has plans to ensure that everyone has a chance to work with those things.

Teachers should be aware of the things students find appealing and have plans to ensure that everyone has a chance to work with those things.

Two analogies come to mind for what it means to lead young people in a shared vision, even as a good bit of "management" is taking place. One analogy is that of effective parents who want their children to develop a keen sense of family. As is the case with most families today, these parents and children are involved in a great deal of schedule shuffling, preparing meals, cleaning house, and so on. But around all the daily aspects of life, the parents take care to build in conversations about family, to ensure that the children understand what the family stands for, to understand what it means to care for one another, and to build shared memories and shared goals. While those conversations seldom take a huge amount of time, they are critical to having a family unit with common and solid underpinnings. They are essential to helping young people develop a sense of what this family is and how a family should be.

A second analogy comes from effective coaching. All coaches spend a great deal of time with the team on game plans and drills and uniforms and exercise. Nonetheless, there has probably never been a great coach who did not make time to build a sense of team. In small moments, in moments of opportunity, in moments of crisis, a great coach leads players in understanding what it means to be part of a team, how a good team works to make every member better, and why it is a matter of pride to be part of this team.

Likewise, a teacher who leads an effectively differentiated classroom spends a great deal of time with students on content, projects, feedback, and the dozens of other things that necessarily take center stage in a classroom. However, the teacher is also consistently aware of helping students understand why this classroom matters, why each student is important in it, how it works to serve each student well, why it is worth their joint efforts, and why it is a matter of pride to be a part of this team.

Some Guidelines for Managing a Differentiated Classroom

Teachers who are good leaders of students do not just do a job. They rally students around what is actually one of life's great missions: growing up to be a learner and to be a productive and contributing member of a circle of friends, a family, and society. That is a cause worth taking seriously; it should be a matter of pride. Nonetheless, a flexible or differentiated classroom still has a management aspect that must be addressed, and understanding how such a class might effectively proceed is part of the teacher's role. In this section, we offer some guidelines that may be helpful to teachers who are working toward developing an orderly-flexible classroom.

Use Anchor Activities

Anchor activities are assignments to which students automatically move when they complete an initial assignment. Students almost never finish an assignment in unison. In fact, that will not even be an aspiration in a differentiated classroom that acknowledges that students will need different amounts of time to complete tasks. Anchor activities are important in a differentiated classroom for at least two reasons. First, students should always have productive work to do. Time is too short and too important to waste. Second, even well-meaning students tend to revert to their "lesser selves" when they have too much time on their hands.

Anchor activities *should* be:

- Focused on the knowledge, understanding, and/or skills that are essential to the topic or discipline (they should provide sense)

- Important and worthy of a student's time and effort (they should have meaning)

- Interesting enough to warrant the student's attention and effort (they should stimulate motivation)

Anchor activities *should not* be:

- "Fluffy" (activities that are not interesting)

- Drill-and-kill exercises (activities that are not motivating)

- Seen as punitive (activities that generate resentment)

- Graded (activities that raise anxiety)

Students should be expected to complete anchor activities. Teachers may want to note whether students move to them when they complete assigned tasks and whether they work with them effectively. These behaviors might be taken into account when reporting on a student's work habits. Teachers should not feel compelled to put a grade on anchor activities.

Consider Using Assigned or Home-Base Seats

Students will often move to different places in the room to work with a partner, work with a group, or find a quiet place to work. Nonetheless, having students begin and end a class period or segment in an assigned seat makes it possible for the teacher to arrange students in predictable and productive ways for whole-class and individual tasks. It also makes it quicker and easier to take attendance, helps teachers distribute materials more efficiently, and makes cleaning up at the end of a class period more effective.

Set Basic Parameters

There are certain baseline expectations that benefit many differentiated classrooms. The teacher needs to help students arrive at an understanding of what these are, why they are important, and how they should work. It is fine to revisit the expectations if they become unnecessary over time or to revise them if they are not working effectively. However, it is critical to have them in place as differentiation begins, to review them as necessary, and to have brief conversations about the degree to which they are working. Baseline expectations will often address the following issues:

- Movement in the room—We know that movement can be an important component in learning and remembering. When is it okay for students to get up and move? When is it not okay? What does it mean to move about the room appropriately? Why do those things matter?

- Noise levels—We know that talking with peers about new learning can help learners make sense and establish meaning. What is the difference between working quietly and working silently? Why does it matter to distinguish between the two? What should students do if noise is bothering them? What signals will the teacher use to remind students to monitor their conversation levels? What should students do when they hear or see those signals?

- When the teacher is off-limits—Establishing that the teacher will be unavailable for questions and comments while students are moving from group to group or place to place in the classroom can be helpful. It allows the teacher to move around the room and ensure smooth transitions rather than be sidelined by conversations. It is very important for the teacher to be off-limits when teaching a small group.

- Handling materials and supplies—If it is important for certain materials to be returned to the same locations every time, certain materials or equipment to be handled in particular ways, furniture to be arranged at the beginning or end of a class or day, and so on, then the teacher should be sure students understand what the expectations are and why they matter.

- Routines for handling paperwork—In differentiated classrooms, students will sometimes complete tasks at different times or even have different tasks. The teacher should designate places where students should turn in particular work when it is completed.

- Group work—Working effectively with a group can be a challenge at any age (including for adult teachers), yet the ability to work collaboratively is likely to be essential for students as they move into an increasingly complex and interdisciplinary world. Teaching students to work effectively with peers may well be as important as any other skill we help them develop. It is good to tell them honestly that collaboration can be both complicated and rewarding. Students need to learn to monitor their own roles in a group and to develop skills of redirecting a group when it is functioning ineffectively. Cooperative learning strategies, when properly implemented, can be very helpful in managing group work.

Develop Methods for Assigning Students to Groups

In a differentiated classroom, flexible grouping is a nonnegotiable. That means that students will work in a variety of groups in a relatively short span of time. Teachers must be able to designate work groups in a way that is easy for them to prepare, easy for students to follow, and efficient in terms of time. Among effective ways of assigning students to groups are the following:

- Using the computer or an overhead projector to project names on a screen that have been arranged by color (the orange group will sit in the area at the front of the room . . .); by category (the Whigs will sit on the right side of the room, the Tories on the left side); or by letter or number (group W will sit up by my desk, group X will sit by the bookshelf in the back of the room, group Y will sit near the computer station . . .). It is helpful to vary the designations over time so that no group is associated with or defined by a designation.

- Using a task chart on which students' names are listed under tasks for a given day and time. Students typically rotate among the tasks over time, but teachers can vary the amount of time particular students work with a particular task, the nature of the task for a group or individual, and the makeup of the groups.

- Projecting a room chart or seating chart with names on it. In this instance, students look for their names on the diagram and move to the places where their names are listed when prompted to do so.

- Preassigning groups. Although some student groupings will need to be fluid, there may be times when it makes sense to have a group that is fixed, or nearly so, for a week or a month. A science teacher may have standing lab groups for a unit. An elementary teacher may have students reading novels based on interest, and those interest-based groups will stay together for three weeks. A mathematics teacher may have mixed-ability review teams that meet together every three or four days during a given unit to make sure everyone understands important concepts and skills. It is efficient to let students know who is in their preassigned groups and for about how long. Then all the teacher needs to say is, "The *Separate Peace* Group should sit at the round table today. The *Wrinkle in Time* Group will sit in the independent study area to continue their individual reading," or "Lab teams 3 and 4 will work at the rear station today," or "The Thursday writing reviewers will meet with me."

Exercise 8.1 (page 185) offers some guidelines for teachers as they think about supporting effective group work.

Develop Methods for Giving Directions for Multiple Tasks

Different teachers, of course, are comfortable with different approaches to directions. When giving directions for multiple tasks that will take place at the same time, it is imperative to ensure that students know precisely what to do and what quality work will look like. Giving directions aloud to the whole class may not be the best approach. Some effective ways of giving directions for multiple tasks include the following:

- Placing task cards in various sections of the room in which students will work. The cards specify clearly what the task is, what students will need to include to ensure quality work, and what procedure the students should follow.

- Appointing student direction providers. The student direction providers are prepared to explain or demonstrate what the students in their group will be doing and what will be necessary for the group to complete the work at a high level of quality.

- Recording directions for group work in a format that does not require the whole class to hear the directions. Audio-recorded directions are especially helpful when a task is complex and would require lengthy written directions, when students are too young to read well, or when older students have difficulty reading.

Develop Procedures for Students to Get Help When the Teacher Is Busy

Although the teacher must be able to work with individuals and small groups for short periods without interruption, it is not acceptable for a student to have to sit and wait in uncertainty for a block of time until a teacher becomes available. The following strategies address the teacher's need to be off-limits at some times and the students' need to get help when they feel stuck:

- Making sure that students learn to listen carefully to assignments and ask questions as instructions are given

- Encouraging students to serve as colleagues to one another and teaching them appropriate ways to request and get help from peers

- Designating an expert of the day who will be available for specific kinds of help

- Ensuring that models of student work, cue cards that remind students how to do particular tasks, and other visual forms of guidance are readily available in the room

Leading and Managing Successfully

There are no infallible recipes for leading students or for managing the details of a classroom. Success in leadership, however, arises from a belief that learning is a profoundly important endeavor and from a commitment to teach so that all children achieve in a way that extends their potential. Success is more likely to occur when the teacher and students work together with a sense of trust and shared purpose. Success in management stems from envisioning what a smoothly functioning classroom would look like and then investing the time and care to plan for and systematically attend to the myriad of details necessary to maintain an orderly-flexible environment.

A Better Scenario

Mrs. Carson asked her students to complete a best-memory/worst-memory exercise as the year began. Students were to write, draw, or record their memories of a time when they felt successful as a learner in a class and a time when they felt angry or defeated as a learner in a class. She studied the responses carefully, took some notes on what she learned from the exercise about each student, and shared themes from the students' work with them. She asked them to help her develop a list of dos and don'ts to ensure that this class would go into the positive-memory column for each student. She told the students she had a rock-solid belief that every student in the class would succeed and that her job was to work with the students to develop the kind of class where that outcome would be a reality.

As the year evolved, she and her students discussed the ways in which they learned best and the ways she might develop assignments that would allow for various approaches to learning. They decided what avenues made sense for the teacher and student to follow when a student was having difficulty with the course content or when a student already knew the content. They looked together for ways to connect what they were learning with the world beyond the classroom. They talked about what "fair" would mean in their classroom. They even talked about ways for grades to play a more positive role in their learning than had sometimes been the case.

Students in the class had little difficulty accepting differentiation because they helped develop the concept of a classroom that worked for everyone. They pitched in with making the classroom run smoothly because it made sense to do so. At the end of the year, one student wrote, "I never knew there were so many ways to learn. I never knew there were ways that would work for me. I never knew teachers thought so much about teaching. I never thought so much about learning, either."

Conclusion

The two of us who wrote this book appreciate your thinking along with us to this point. However, in writing the book, our hope was not just that readers would finish it, but that it would be helpful to them in the difficult work of making classrooms truly effective for all kinds of learners, especially as our student population becomes more diverse. The status quo is comfortable and appealing, and it does nothing to help us move forward as individuals or as a profession.

What happens next depends not on the authors but on a reader's commitment to personal and professional growth in leading academically and culturally diverse classrooms. Here are a final few suggestions for next steps:

- Study your students. Watch them in order to see the classroom from their perspectives.

- Take notes as they work. Make it a point to learn something new about several students each day. Connect with them. Ask for their input toward making the class work well for them. Follow their lead.

- Take your next step. Just as is the case with each of your students, you have a next step that you must take in order to grow toward your maximum potential. Recognize that there is a growing body of knowledge about how the brain learns, and think seriously about what that next step is for you.

- Set a specific goal for yourself in becoming a more academically responsive teacher. Set a timeline for steps in reaching that goal. Stick with the plan.

- Start small. Ensure you have a brain-friendly classroom, and begin differentiating in just one class or one subject. Differentiate at the beginning of a class period or at the end. Try out just one strategy.

- Differentiate just one element in your classroom. Differentiate projects, provide a broader array of materials, or use small groups for targeted instruction.

- Work with colleagues. Ask your grade-level peers or your department colleagues to team with you in planning and carrying out the plans for ensuring a brain-friendly environment that supports differentiation. Team up with specialists in your school, such as teachers of English learners; special education, reading, or gifted education teachers; and counselors. Learn together. Share materials, lesson plans, strategies, and management plans. Troubleshoot together. Share successes.

A great piece of advice that a colleague shared with us is to avoid confusing the edge of our ruts with the horizon. We hope we have clarified the horizon in terms of what it means to differentiate instruction successfully in ways that are consistent with current brain research and why that matters. In a profession that can easily become "rut-bound," keep your eye on the horizon. What comes next is *your* call.

Exercise 8.1

Some Guidelines for Teachers for Effective Group Work

Consider the following guidelines as you plan for group work in your differentiated classroom. If you are a teacher, consider the degree to which these statements typify your work with student groups. If you are an administrator, think about the degree to which teachers consistently apply these principles in their work with student groups. In both cases, note specific items that are worthy of further thought, discussion, or formal professional development. Use the questions in faculty meetings, grade-level meetings, or department meetings to talk about ways in which teachers can support effective group work in their classrooms.

1. All students in the group should understand the task goals and directions.

2. All students in the group should understand what is expected of individuals to make the group work well.

3. The task students are asked to do in the group must be aligned with the task goals (must lead students to what they should know, understand, and be able to do).

4. The students should find the task interesting.

5. The task should require an important contribution from each individual and should be structured in such a way that all students can access important ideas and materials and all students have an appropriate way to express their learning. (The task should not be structured so that some students can contribute to the success of the effort but others cannot.)

6. The task should be appropriately challenging for the group.

7. The task should require genuine collaboration to achieve shared understanding. (It should not be possible for some students to do the work and others to remain disengaged.)

8. The timelines for the group's work should be brisk (but not rigid).

9. There should be opportunities for teacher or peer coaching and in-process quality checks to support the success of the group and the individuals in it.

10. Each individual in the group should be accountable for his or her own understanding of all elements in the task.

11. Students should understand what to do to support one another's success.

12. Students should understand what to do when the group is not working effectively.

13. Students should understand what to do when they complete their work at a high level of quality.

14. There should be a "way out" for students who are not succeeding with the group. That is, there should be a procedure for having a student exit a group when he or she is persistently disruptive to the group or the group is consistently problematic for the student. The exit strategy should not be punitive but should allow the student to continue working productively in another context. The teacher should arrange to work with the student over time to resolve the issues that have caused the difficulty so that the student will be better able to work collaboratively and productively with peers.

References

Amabile, T. (1983). *The social psychology of creativity*. New York: Springer-Verlag.

Amabile, T. (1996). *Creativity in context*. Boulder, CO: Westview Press.

Anderson, R., & Pavan, B. (1993). *Nongradedness: Helping it to happen*. Lancaster, PA: Technomic.

Asher, J. J. (2007). *Mathematics for everyone: Recommendations from a prize-winner in math education*. Accessed at www.tpr-world.com/math_for_everyone.pdf on May 19, 2010.

Bender, W. N. (2003). *Relational discipline: Strategies for in-your-face kids*. Boston: Allyn & Bacon.

Besançon, M., & Lubart, T. (2008). Differences in the development of creative competencies in children schooled in diverse learning environments. *Learning and Individual Differences, 18*(4), 381–389.

Brambati, S. M., Renda, N. C., Rankin, K. P., Rosen, H. J., Seeley, W. W., Ashburner, J., et al. (2007). A tensor based morphometry study of longitudinal gray matter contraction in FTD. *NeuroImage, 35*(3), 998–1003.

Bridgeland, J. M., DiIulio, J. J., Jr., & Morison, K. B. (2006). *The silent epidemic: Perspectives of high school dropouts*. Washington, DC: Civic Enterprises.

Brooks, R., & Goldstein, S. (2008). The mindset of teachers capable of fostering resilience in students. *Canadian Journal of School Psychology, 23*, 114–126.

Bruner, J. (1961). The act of discovery. *Harvard Educational Review, 31*(1), 21–32.

Buchanan, T. W., & Tranel, D. (2008). Stress and emotional memory retrieval: Effects of sex and cortisol response. *Neurobiology of Learning and Memory, 89*, 134–141.

Burke, L. A., & Williams, J. M. (2008). Developing young thinkers: An intervention aimed to enhance children's thinking skills. *Thinking Skills and Creativity, 3*, 104–124.

Caine, R. N., Caine, G., McClintic, C., & Klimek, K. (2005). *12 brain/mind learning principles in action: The fieldbook for making connections, teaching, and the human brain*. Thousand Oaks, CA: Corwin Press.

Carbonaro, W., & Gamoran, A. (2002). The production of achievement inequality in high school English. *American Educational Research Journal, 39,* 801–827.

Carroll, A., Houghton, S., Wood, R., Unsworth, K., Hattie, J., Gordon, L., et al. (2009). Self-efficacy and academic achievement in Australian high school students: The mediating effects of academic aspirations and delinquency. *Journal of Adolescence, 32,* 797–817.

Carter, R. (1998). *Mapping the mind.* Los Angeles: University of California Press.

CAST. (2008). *Universal design for learning guidelines 1.0.* Accessed at www.cast.org/publications/UDLguidelines/version1.html on July 5, 2009.

Chan, J. C. K. (2009). When does retrieval induce forgetting and when does it induce facilitation? Implications for retrieval inhibition, testing effect, and text processing. *Journal of Memory and Language, 61,* 153–170.

Chen, I. (2009, June). Brain cells for socializing: Does an obscure nerve cell explain what gorillas, elephants, whales—and people—have in common? *Smithsonian,* 38–43.

Clements, A., (2004). *The report card.* New York: Simon & Schuster.

Collins, M. A., & Amabile, T. (1999). Motivation and creativity. In R. J. Sternberg (Ed.), *Handbook of creativity* (pp. 297–312). New York: Cambridge University Press.

Colunga, E., & Smith, L. B. (2008). Flexibility and variability: Essential to human cognition and the study of human cognition. *New Ideas in Psychology, 26,* 174–192.

Cowan, N. (2001). The magical number 4 in short-term memory: A reconsideration of mental storage capacity. *Behavioral and Brain Sciences, 24*(1), 87–114.

Csikszentmihalyi, M., Rathunde, K., & Whalen, S. (1993). *Talented teenagers: The roots of success and failure.* New York: Cambridge University Press.

Curry, L. (1990). A critique of the research on learning styles. *Educational Leadership, 42*(2), 50–56.

Darling-Hammond, L., Bransford, J., LePage, P., & Hammerness, K. (Eds.). (2005). *Preparing teachers for a changing world: What teachers should learn and be able to do.* San Francisco: Jossey-Bass.

de Bono, E. (1985). *Six thinking hats.* New York: Little, Brown.

Delis, D. C., Lansing, A., Houston, W. S., Wetter, S., Han, S. D., Jacobson, M., et al. (2007). Creativity lost: The importance of testing higher-level executive functions in school-age children and adolescents. *Journal of Psychoeducational Assessment, 25*(1), 29–40.

Demetriadis, S. N., Papadopoulos, P. M., Stamelos, I. G., & Fischer, F. (2008). The effect of scaffolding students' context-generating cognitive activity in technology-enhanced case-based learning. *Computers & Education, 51,* 939–954.

Dewey, J. (1938). *Experience and education.* Indianapolis, IN: Kappa Delta Pi.

Diamond, A. (2009). All or none hypothesis: A global-default mode that characterizes the brain and mind. *Developmental Psychology, 45,* 130–138.

Dunn, R., & Dunn, K. (1993). *Teaching secondary students through their individual learning styles: Practical approaches for grades 7–12.* Boston: Allyn & Bacon.

Dweck, C. S. (2006). *Mindset: The new psychology of success.* New York: Random House.

Earl, L. (2003). *Assessment as learning: Using classroom assessment to maximize student learning.* Thousand Oaks, CA: Corwin Press.

Elfers, A., Plecki, M., & Knapp, M. (2006). Teacher mobility: Looking more closely at "the movers" within a state system. *Peabody Journal of Education, (81)*3, 94–127.

Eliot, L. (2009). *Pink brain, blue brain: How small differences grow into troublesome gaps—and what we can do about it.* New York: Houghton Mifflin Harcourt.

Engelmann, J. B., & Pessoa, L. (2007). Motivation sharpens exogenous spatial attention. *Emotion, 7*(4), 668–674.

Erickson, H. L. (2007). *Concept-based curriculum and instruction for the thinking classroom.* Thousand Oaks, CA: Corwin Press.

Erickson, H. L. (2008). *Stirring the head, heart, and soul: Redefining curriculum, instruction, and concept-based learning* (3rd ed.). Thousand Oaks, CA: Corwin Press.

Ferguson, R. (2002). *Who doesn't meet the eye: Understanding and addressing racial disparities in high achieving suburban schools.* Naperville, IL: North Central Regional Educational Laboratory.

Fink, A., Benedek, M., Grabner, R. H., Staudt, B., & Neubauer, A. C. (2007). Creativity meets neuroscience: Experimental tasks for the neuroscientific study of creative thinking. *Methods, 42*(1), 68–76.

Fisher, C., Berliner, D., Filby, N., Marliave, R., Cahen, L., & Dishaw, M. (1980). Teaching behaviors, academic learning time, and student achievement: An overview. In C. Denham & A. Lieberman (Eds.), *Time to learn* (pp. 7–32). Washington, DC: National Institutes of Education.

Forstmann, B. U., Brass, M., Koch, I., & von Cramon, D. Y. (2006). Voluntary selection of task sets revealed by functional magnetic resonance imaging. *Journal of Cognitive Neuroscience, 18,* 388–398.

Friedman, D., Goldman, R., Stern, Y., & Brown, T. R. (2009). The brain's orienting response: An event-related functional magnetic resonance imaging investigation. *Human Brain Mapping, 30,* 1144–1154.

Fulk, B., & Montgomery-Grymes, D. (1994). Strategies to improve student motivation. *Intervention in School and Clinic, 30,* 28–33.

Gardner, H. (2004). *Frames of mind: The theory of multiple intelligences* (20th anniversary ed.). New York: Basic Books. (Original work published 1983)

Gardner, H. (2006). *Multiple intelligences: New horizons in theory and practice* (Rev. ed.). New York: Basic Books.

Garn, C. L., Allen, M. D., & Larsen, J. D. (2009). An fMRI study of sex differences in brain activation during object naming. *Cortex, 45,* 610–618.

Gay, G. (2000). *Culturally responsive teaching: Theory, research, and practice.* New York: Teachers College Press.

Gayfer, M. (1991). *The multi-grade classroom: Myth and reality—A Canadian study.* Toronto, ON: Canadian Education Association.

Gee, J. P. (2007). *What video games have to teach us about learning and literacy* (2nd ed.). New York: Palgrave Macmillan.

Ginsberg, M. & Wlodkowski, R. (2000). *Creating highly motivating classrooms for all students: A schoolwide approach to powerful teaching with diverse learners.* San Francisco: Jossey-Bass.

Glassner, A., & Schwarz, B. B. (2007). What stands and develops between creative and critical thinking? Argumentation? *Thinking Skills and Creativity, 2*(1), 10–18.

Goldberg, E. (2001). *The executive brain: Frontal lobes and the civilized mind.* New York: Oxford University Press.

Goode, P. E., Goddard, P. H., & Pascual-Leone, J. (2002). Event-related potentials index cognitive style differences during a serial-order recall task. *International Journal of Psychophysiology, 43,* 123–140.

Gottfried, A. E., & Gottfried, A. W. (1996). A longitudinal study of academic intrinsic motivation in intellectually gifted children: Childhood through early adolescence. *Gifted Child Quarterly, 40,* 179–183.

Gray, J., & Thomas, H. (2005). *If she only knew me.* Owensboro, KY: Rocket.

Gregorc, A. F. (1979). Learning/teaching styles: Potent forces behind them. *Educational Leadership, 36,* 234–236.

Guskey, T. (2007). Using assessments to improve teaching *and* learning. In D. Reeves (Ed.), *Ahead of the curve: The power of assessment to transform teaching and learning* (pp. 15–29). Bloomington, IN: Solution Tree Press.

Hall P. S., & Hall, N. D. (2003, September). Building relationships with challenging children. *Educational Leadership, 61,* 60–63.

Haynes, J.-D., Sakai, K., Rees, G., Gilbert, S., Frith, C., & Passingham, R. E. (2007). Reading hidden intentions in the human brain. *Current Biology, 17,* 323–328.

Hébert, T. (1993). Reflections at graduation: The long-term impact of elementary school experiences in creative productivity. *Roeper Review, 16*(1), 22–28.

Hidi. S. (1990). Interest and its contribution as a mental resource for learning. *Review of Educational Research, 60,* 549–571.

Hidi, S., & Anderson, V. (1992). Situational interest and its impact on reading and expository writing. In K. A. Renninger, S. Hidi, & A. Krapp (Eds.), *The role of interest in learning and development* (pp. 215–238). Hillsdale, NJ: Lawrence Erlbaum.

Hidi, S., & Berndorff, D. (1998). Situational interest and learning. In L. Hoffmann, A. Krapp, K. A. Renninger, & J. Baumert (Eds.), *Interest and learning: Proceedings of the Seeon conference on interest and gender* (pp. 74–90). Kiel, Germany: IPN.

Holland, R. P. (1982). Learner characteristics and learner performance: Implications for instructional placement decisions. *Journal of Special Education, 16*(1), 7–20.

Hunt, D. (1971). *Matching models in education: The coordination of teaching methods with student characteristics* (Monograph #10). Toronto: Ontario Institute for Studies in Education.

Jensen, A. R. (1998). *The g factor: The science of mental ability.* Westport, CT: Praeger.

Johnson, K., & Becker, A. (2010). *Whole brain atlas.* Accessed at www.med .harvard.edu/AANLIB/home.html on May 19, 2010.

Kajder, S. (2006). *Bringing the outside in: Visual ways to engage reluctant readers.* Portland, ME: Stenhouse.

Kaplan, F., & Oudeyer, P. Y. (2007). In search of the neural circuits of intrinsic motivation. *Frontiers in Neuroscience, 1*, 225–236.

Karpicke, J. D., & Zaromb, F. M. (2010). Retrieval mode distinguishes the testing effect from the generation effect. *Journal of Memory and Language, 62*, 227–239.

Keller, K., & Menon, V. (2009). Gender differences in the functional and structural neuroanatomy of mathematical cognition. *NeuroImage, 47*, 342–352.

Knapp, M. S., Shields, P. M., & Turnbull, B. J. (1992). *Academic challenge for children of poverty: Summary report.* Washington, DC: U.S. Department of Education Office of Policy and Planning.

Kolb, D. (1984). *Experiential learning: Experience as the source of learning and development.* Englewood Cliffs, NJ: Prentice Hall.

Kumaran, D., & Maguire, E. A. (2007). Match-mismatch processes underlie human hippocampal responses to associative novelty. *Journal of Neuroscience, 27*, 8517–8524.

Ladson-Billings, G. (1994). *The dreamkeepers: Successful teachers of African American children.* San Francisco: Jossey-Bass.

Lau, H. C., Rogers, R. D., Haggard, P., & Passingham, R. E. (2004). Attention to intention. *Science, 303*(5661), 1208–1210.

Levy, S. (1996). *Starting from scratch: One classroom builds its own curriculum.* Portsmouth, NH: Heinemann.

Lortie, D. (2002). *Schoolteacher: A sociological study* (2nd ed.). Chicago: University of Chicago Press.

Maguire, E. A., Frith, C. D., & Morris, R. G. M. (1999). The functional neuroanatomy of comprehension and memory: The importance of prior knowledge. *Brain, 122*, 1839–1850.

Marzano, R. J., Marzano J. S., & Pickering, D. (2003). *Classroom management that works: Research-based strategies for every teacher.* Alexandria, VA: Association for Supervision and Curriculum Development.

Maslow, A. (1943). A theory of human motivation. *Psychological Review, 50,* 370–396.

McAllister, G., & Irvine, J. J. (2002). The role of empathy in teaching culturally diverse students: A qualitative study of teachers' beliefs. *Journal of Teacher Education, 53*(5), 433–443.

McCarthy, B. (1987). *4-MAT: Teaching to learning styles.* Barrington, IL: EXCEL.

McKay, M. T., Fischler, I., & Dunn, B. R. (2002). Cognitive style and recall of text: An EEG analysis. *Learning and Individual Differences, 14*(1), 1–21.

McQuillan, P. J. (2005). Possibilities and pitfalls: A comparative analysis of student empowerment. *American Educational Research Journal, 42,* 639–670.

Miller, B. (1990). A review of the quantitative research on multigrade instruction. *Research in Rural Education, 7,* 1–8.

Miller, G. A. (1956). The magical number seven, plus-or-minus two: Some limits on our capacity for processing information. *Psychological Review, 101,* 343–352.

Mitchell, J. P., Banaji, M. R., & Macrae, C. N. (2005). The link between social cognition and self-referential thought in the medial prefrontal cortex. *Journal of Cognitive Neuroscience, 17,* 1306–1315.

Mizuno, K., Tanaka, M., Ishii, A., Tanabe, H. C., Onoe, H., Sadato, N., et al. (2008). The neural basis of academic achievement motivation. *NeuroImage, 42,* 369–378.

Moore, D. W., Bhadelia, R. A., Billings, R. L., Fulwiler, C., Heilman, K. M., Rood, K. M., et al. (2009). Hemispheric connectivity and the visual-spatial divergent-thinking component of creativity. *Brain and Cognition, 70*(3), 267–272.

National Research Council. (1999). *How people learn: Brain, mind, experience, and school.* Washington, DC: National Academy Press.

National Research Council. (2001). *Knowing what students know: The science and design of educational assessment.* Washington, DC: National Academies Press.

Neitzel, C., Alexander, J. M., & Johnson, K. E. (2008). Children's early interest-based activities in the home and subsequent information contributions and pursuits in kindergarten. *Journal of Educational Psychology, 100,* 782–797.

Oberauer, K., & Kliegl, R. (2006). A formal model of capacity limits in working memory. *Journal of Memory and Language, 55,* 601–626.

Ochsner, K. N. (2007). Social cognitive neuroscience: Historic development, core principles, and future promise. In A. W. Kruglanski & E. Tory (Eds.), *Social psychology: Handbook of basic principles* (2nd ed., pp. 39–68). New York: Guilford Press.

O'Connor, K. (2007). *A repair kit for grading: 15 fixes for broken grades.* Portland, OR: Educational Testing Service.

O'Connor, K. (2009). *How to grade for learning, K–12* (3rd ed.). Thousand Oaks, CA: Corwin Press.

Okuhata, S. T., Okazaki, S., & Maekawa, H. (2009). EEG coherence pattern during simultaneous and successive processing tasks. *International Journal of Psychophysiology, 72*(2), 89–96.

Olson, I. R., Plotzker, A., & Ezzyat, Y., (2007). The enigmatic temporal pole: A review of findings on social and emotional processing. *Brain, 130*, 1718–1731.

Peelle, J. E., Troiani, V., & Grossman, M. (2009). Interaction between process and content in semantic memory: An fMRI study of noun feature knowledge. *Neuropsychologia, 47*, 995–1003.

Petersen, J. (2009). "This test makes no freaking sense": Criticism, confusion, and frustration in timed writing. *Assessing Writing, 14*(3), 178–193.

Rao, H., Betancourt, L., Giannetta, J. M., Brodsky, N. L., Korczykowski, M., Avants, B. B., et al. (2010). Early parental care is important for hippocampal maturation: Evidence from brain morphology in humans. *NeuroImage, 49*, 1144–1150.

Raymond, J. (2009). Interactions of attention, emotion and motivation. *Progress in Brain Research, 176*, 293–308.

Reeves, D. (2000). Standards are not enough: Essential transformations for school success. *NASSP Bulletin, 84*(620), 5–19.

Reeves, D. (Ed.). (2007). *Ahead of the curve: The power of assessment to transform teaching and learning.* Bloomington, IN: Solution Tree Press.

Renninger, K. A. (1990). Children's play interests, representation and activity. In R. Fivush & J. Hudson (Eds.), *Knowing and remembering in young children* (pp. 127–165). New York: Cambridge University Press.

Renninger, K. A. (1998). The roles of individual interest(s) and gender in learning: An overview-of-research on preschool and elementary school-aged children/students. In L. Hoffmann, A. Krapp, K. A. Renninger, & J. Baumert (Eds.), *Interest and learning: Proceedings of the Seeon conference on interest and gender* (pp. 165–175). Kiel, Germany: IPN.

Riding, R., & Rayner, S. (1997). Towards a categorisation of cognitive styles and learning styles. *Educational Psychology, 17*(1–2), 5–27.

Robins, K. N., Lindsey, R., Lindsey, D., & Terrell, R. (2002). *Culturally proficient instruction: A guide for people who teach.* Thousand Oaks, CA: Corwin Press.

Sadler-Smith, E. (2001). A reply to Reynolds's critique of learning style. *Management Learning, 32*, 291–304.

Salomone, R. (2003). *Same, different, equal: Rethinking single-sex schooling.* New Haven, CT: Yale University Press.

Sandi, C. & Pinelo-Nava, M. T. (2007). Stress and memory: Behavioral effects and neurobiological mechanisms. *Neural Plasticity, 2007*, 1–20. Accessed at www.ncbi.nlm.nih.gov/pmc/articles/PMC1950232/?tool=pmcentrez on April 6, 2010.

Sax, L. (2005). *Why gender matters: What parents and teachers need to know about the emerging science of sex differences.* New York: Broadway Books.

Schmithorst, V. J., & Holland, S. K. (2007). Sex differences in the development of neuroanatomical functional connectivity underlying intelligence found using Bayesian connectivity analysis. *NeuroImage, 35,* 406–419.

Sharan, Y., & Sharan, S. (1992). *Expanding cooperative learning through group investigation.* New York: Teachers College Press.

Shaw, P., Greenstein, D., Lerch, J., Clasen, L., Lenroot, R., Gogtay, N., et al. (2006). Intellectual ability and cortical development in children and adolescents. *Nature, 440,* 676–679.

Shaywitz, B. A., Shaywitz, S. E., Pugh, K. R., Constable, R. T., Skudlarski, P., Fulbright, R. K., et al. (1995). Sex differences in the functional organization of the brain for language. *Nature, 373,* 607–609.

Sousa, D. (2006). *How the brain learns* (3rd ed.). Thousand Oaks, CA: Corwin Press.

Sousa, D. (2009). *How the brain influences behavior: Management strategies for every classroom.* Thousand Oaks, CA: Corwin Press.

Squire, L. R., & Kandel, E. R. (1999). *Memory: From mind to molecules.* New York: W. H. Freeman.

Sternberg, R. (1985). *Beyond IQ: A triarchic theory of human intelligence.* New York: Cambridge University Press.

Stiggins, R. (2001). *Student-involved classroom assessment* (3rd ed.). Upper Saddle River, NJ: Merrill Prentice Hall.

Stipek, D. (2006, September). Relationships matter. *Educational Leadership, 64,* 46–49.

Storm, E. E., & Tecott, L. H. (2005). Social circuits: Peptidergic regulation of mammalian social behavior. *Neuron, 47,* 483–486.

Storti, C. (1999). *Figuring foreigners out: A practical guide.* Yarmouth, ME: Intercultural Press.

Tierney, R. D. & Charland, J. (2007, April). *Stocks and prospects: Research on formative assessment in secondary classrooms.* Paper presented at the annual meeting of the American Educational Research Association, Chicago.

Tobias, S. (1994). Interest, prior knowledge, and learning. *Review of Educational Research, 64,* 37–54.

Tomlinson, C. A. (1999). *The differentiated classroom: Responding to the needs of all learners.* Alexandria, VA: Association for Supervision and Curriculum Development.

Tomlinson, C. A. (2001). *How to differentiate instruction in mixed-ability classrooms* (2nd ed.). Alexandria, VA: Association for Supervision and Curriculum Development.

Tomlinson, C. A. (2003). *Fulfilling the promise of the differentiated classroom: Strategies and tools for responsive teaching.* Alexandria, VA: Association for Supervision and Curriculum Development.

Tomlinson, C. A., Brighton, C., Hertberg, H., Callahan, C. M., Moon, T. R., Brimijoin, K., et al. (2003). Differentiating instruction in response to student readiness, interest, and learning profile in academically diverse classrooms: A review of literature. *Journal for the Education of the Gifted, 27*(2–3), 119–145.

Tomlinson, C. A., Kaplan, S., Renzulli, J., Purcell, J., Leppien, J., Burns, D., et al. (2008). *The parallel curriculum: A design to develop learner potential and challenge advanced learners.* Thousand Oaks, CA: Corwin Press.

Tomlinson, C. A., & McTighe, J. (2006). *Integrating differentiated instruction and understanding by design: Connecting content and kids.* Alexandria, VA: Association for Supervision and Curriculum Development.

Tompkins, J. (1996). *A life in school: What the teacher learned.* New York: Perseus.

Torrance, E. P. (1995). Insights about creativity: Questioned, rejected, ridiculed, ignored. *Educational Psychology Review, 7*(3), 313–322.

Trumbull, E., Rothstein-Fisch, C., Greenfield, P., & Quiroz, B. (2001). *Bridging cultures between home and school: A guide for teachers.* Mahwah, NJ: Lawrence Erlbaum.

Tsui, J. M., & Mazzocco, M. M. M. (2007). Effects of math anxiety and perfectionism on timed versus untimed math testing in mathematically gifted sixth graders. *Roeper Review, 29*(2), 132–139.

Tynjälä, P. (2008). Perspectives into learning at the workplace. *Educational Research Review, 3*(2), 130–154.

Vansteenkiste, M., Simons, J., Lens, W., Sheldon, K. M., & Deci, E. L. (2004). Motivating learning, performance, and persistence: The synergistic effects of intrinsic goal contents and autonomy-supportive contexts. *Journal of Personality and Social Psychology, 87,* 246–260.

Vollmeyer, R., & Rheinberg, F. (2000). Does motivation affect performance via persistence? *Learning and Instruction, 10*(4), 293–309.

Vygotsky, L. S. (1978). *Mind in society: The development of higher psychological processes.* Cambridge, MA: Harvard University Press.

Wagner, T. (2008). *The global achievement gap: Why even our best schools don't teach the new survival skills our children need—and what we can do about it.* New York: Basic Books.

Walqui, A. (2000). *Access and engagement: Program design and instructional approaches for immigrant students in secondary school.* McHenry, IL: Center for Applied Linguistics and Delta Systems.

Whalen, S. (1998). Flow and engagement of talent: Implications for secondary schooling. *NASSP Bulletin, 82*(595), 22–37.

Wiggins, G. (1993). *Assessing student performance: Exploring the purpose and limits of testing.* San Francisco: Jossey-Bass.

Wiggins, G. (1998). *Educative assessment: Designing assessments to inform and improve student performance.* San Francisco: Jossey-Bass.

Wiggins, G., & McTighe, J. (2005). *Understanding by Design* (2nd ed.). Alexandria, VA: Association for Supervision and Curriculum Development.

Wilke, M., Holland, S. K., & Krägeloh-Mann, I. (2007). Global, regional, and local development of gray and white matter volume in normal children. *Experimental Brain Research, 178,* 296–307.

Willingham, D. (2009). *Why don't students like school? A cognitive scientist answers questions about how the mind works and what it means for the classroom.* San Francisco: Jossey-Bass.

Wittmann, B. C., Bunzeck, N., Dolan, R. J., & Düzel, E. (2007). Anticipation of novelty recruits reward system and hippocampus while promoting recollection. *NeuroImage, 38,* 194–202.

Wolf, O. T. (2009). Stress and memory in humans: Twelve years of progress? *Brain Research, 1293,* 142–154.

Index

Mind, Brain, & Education: Neuroscience Implications for the Classroom
Edited by David A. Sousa
Understanding how the brain learns helps teachers do their jobs more effectively. In this book, primary researchers in the emerging field of educational neuroscience share the latest findings on the learning process and address their implications for educational theory and practice.
BKF358

On Excellence in Teaching
Edited by Robert Marzano
Learn from the world's best education researchers, theorists, and staff developers. The authors' diverse expertise delivers a wide range of theories and strategies and provides a comprehensive view of effective instruction from a theoretical, systemic, and classroom perspective.
BKF278

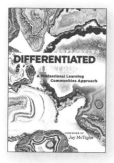

Supporting Differentiated Instruction: A Professional Learning Communities Approach
Robin J. Fogarty and Brian M. Pete
Foreword by Jay McTighe
Examine how PLCs provide the decision-making platform for the rigorous work of differentiated classroom instruction. A practical guide to implementing differentiation in the classroom, this book offers a roadmap to effective teaching that responds to diverse learning needs.
BKF348

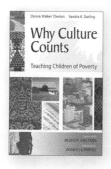

Why Culture Counts: Teaching Children of Poverty
Donna Walker Tileston and Sandra K. Darling
Foreword by Belinda Williams
Afterword by Rosilyn Carroll
Learn how to close the achievement gap by making use of the often-ignored cultural assets inherent to children of poverty and diverse learners. *Why Culture Counts* includes numerous methods for differentiating the context, content, and process of instruction.
BKF255

21st Century Skills: Rethinking How Students Learn
Edited by James Bellanca and Ron Brandt
Examine the Framework for 21st Century Learning from the Partnership for 21st Century Skills as a way to reenvision learning in a rapidly evolving global and technological world. Learn why these skills are necessary, which are most important, and how to best help schools include them.
BKF389

Solution Tree | Press *a division of* Solution Tree

Visit solution-tree.com or call 800.733.6786 to order.